CAMBRIDGE LIBRARY COLLECTION

Books of enduring scholarly value

Travel and Exploration

The history of travel writing dates back to the Bible, Caesar, the Vikings and the Crusaders, and its many themes include war, trade, science and recreation. Explorers from Columbus to Cook charted lands not previously visited by Western travellers, and were followed by merchants, missionaries, and colonists, who wrote accounts of their experiences. The development of steam power in the nineteenth century provided opportunities for increasing numbers of 'ordinary' people to travel further, more economically, and more safely, and resulted in great enthusiasm for travel writing among the reading public. Works included in this series range from first-hand descriptions of previously unrecorded places, to literary accounts of the strange habits of foreigners, to examples of the burgeoning numbers of guidebooks produced to satisfy the needs of a new kind of traveller - the tourist.

Border and Bastille

Published in 1863, English novelist George Alfred Lawrence's first foray into travel-writing recounts a failed attempt to join the Confederate Army of Virginia. Lawrence (1827–76), who abandoned a law career when his first novel (1853) sold, became known for books that celebrated the brash, violent, aristocratic hero. Lawrence had joined the militia in England, and one critic has suggested that Lawrence's American expedition was his attempt to live as his most famous character, Guy Livingstone, and his attempt to write himself into heroism. In novelistic fashion his work describes his voyage from England to New York, his journey as far as Maryland, his capture by farmers, and his weeks in a Washington gaol. Lawrence embraced the Confederate cause and his work, often racist and relativist, expresses total faith in it.

Border and Bastille

by the Author of "Guy Livingstone"

GEORGE ALFRED LAWRENCE

CAMBRIDGE UNIVERSITY PRESS

Cambridge, New York, Melbourne, Madrid, Cape Town,
Singapore, São Paolo, Delhi, Tokyo, Mexico City

Published in the United States of America by Cambridge University Press, New York

www.cambridge.org
Information on this title: www.cambridge.org/9781108033299

© in this compilation Cambridge University Press 2011

This edition first published 1863
This digitally printed version 2011

ISBN 978-1-108-03329-9 Paperback

BORDER AND BASTILLE.

BORDER AND BASTILLE.

BY

THE AUTHOR OF "GUY LIVINGSTONE."

———

LONDON :

TINSLEY BROTHERS, 18, CATHERINE ST., STRAND.

1863.

LONDON:
BRADBURY AND EVANS, PRINTERS, WHITEFRIARS

L'ENVOI.

WHEN, late in last autumn, I determined to start for the Confederate States as soon as necessary preparations could be completed, I had listened not only to my own curiosity, impelling me to see at least one campaign of a war, the like of which this world has never known, but also to the suggestions of those who thought that I might find materials there for a book that would interest many here in England. My intention from the first was to serve as a volunteer-aide in the staff of the army in Virginia, so long as I should find either pen-work or handiwork to do. The South might easily have gained a more efficient recruit ; but a more earnest adherent it would have been hard to find. I do not attempt to disguise the fact that my predilections were thoroughly settled long before I left England; indeed, it is the consciousness of a strong partisan spirit at my heart which has made me strive so hard, not only to state facts as accurately as possible, but to abstain from colouring them with involuntary prejudice.

To say nothing of my being afterwards backed by the powerful Secessionist interest at Baltimore, the introductory letters furnished me by Colonel Dudley Mann and Mr. Slidell, addressed to the most influential personages—civil and military—in the Confederacy, from President Davis downwards, were such as could hardly have failed to secure me the position I desired, though they benevolently over-estimated the qualifications of the bearer. To the first of these gentlemen I am indebted for much kindness and valuable advice; to the second I am personally unknown; and I am glad to have this opportunity of acknowledging his ready courtesy. It was Colonel Mann who counselled my going through the Northern States, instead of attempting to run the blockade from Nassau or Bermuda, as I had originally intended. In spite of the events, I am so certain that the advice was sound and wise, that I do not repent—scarcely regret—having followed it.

I need not particularise the precaution taken to ensure the safe delivery of these credentials : it is sufficient to state that they were never submitted to Federal inspection; nor had I ever at any time in my possession a single document which could vitiate my claim to the rights of a neutral and civilian. Even Mr. Seward did not pretend to refuse liberty of unexpressed sympathy with either side to an utter foreigner. While I was a free agent in the Northern States, I was careful to indulge in no other.

Since my return, I hear that some one has been kind enough to insinuate that I might have succeeded better if I had been more careful to prosecute my journey South with vigour at any risk; or if I had been less imprudent in parading my object while in Baltimore. I prefer to meet the first of these assertions by a simple record of facts, and by the most unqualified denial that it is possible to give to any falsehood, written or spoken. As to the second—really quite as unfounded—it may be well to say, that before I had been a full fortnight in America, I was "posted" in the literary column of "Willis' Home Journal." I could not quarrel with the terms in which the intelligence—avowedly copied from an English paper—was couched. The writer seemed to know rather more about my intentions—if not of my antecedents—than I knew myself; but I can honestly say that the halo of romance with which he was pleased to surround a very practical purpose, did not however compensate me for the inconvenient publicity. This paragraph soon found its way into other journals, and at last confronted me—to my infinite disgust— in the "Baltimore Clipper," a bitter Unionist organ.

Perhaps this will answer sufficiently the accusation of "parade," for even had we been disposed to indulge in an "alarum and flourish of trumpets," the sensation-mongers would have anticipated the absurdity. Besides this, my movements were not in anywise interfered with up to the moment of my arrest, when we were miles beyond all Federal pickets. My captors, of course, had never heard of my existence till we met. It is more than probable that the report just referred to did greatly complicate my position when I was actually in confinement; but here my person—not my plans—suffered, and here, the real mischief of that very involuntary publicity began and ended.

After my plans were finally arranged, I had an interview with the editorial powers of the *Morning Post;* there it was settled that I should communicate to that journal as constantly as circumstances would permit, any interesting matter or incidents that fell in my way, in consideration of which was voted a liberal supplement to the sinews of war; but it was clearly understood that my movements and line of action were to be absolutely untrammelled. I could not have entered into any contract that in any way interfered with the primary object I had in view. I had no intention of commencing such correspondence before I had actually crossed the Southern frontier, so that one letter from Baltimore—afterwards quoted —was the solitary contribution I was able to furnish.

I have said thus much, because I wish any one who may be interested on the point to know clearly on what footing I stood at starting : for the general public, of course, the subject cannot have the slightest interest.

Of all compositions, I suppose, a personal narrative is the most wearying to the writer, if not to the reader ; egotistical talk may be pleasant enough, but, commit it to paper, the fault carries its own punishment. The recurrence of that everlasting first pronoun becomes a real stumbling-block to one at last. Yet there is no evading it, unless you cast your story into a curt, succinct diary : to carry this off effectively, requires a succession of incidents, more varied and important than befell me.

A failure—absolute and complete—however brought

about, is a fair mark for mockery, if not for censure. Perhaps, however, I may hope that some of my readers, in charity, if not in justice, will believe that I have honestly tried to avoid over-colouring details of personal adventure, and that no word here is set down in wilful insincerity or malice, though all are written by one whose enmity to all purely republican institutions will endure to his life's end.

CONTENTS.

BORDER AND BASTILLE.

CHAPTER I.

A FOUL START.

LOOKING back on an experience of many lands and seas, I cannot recall a single scene more utterly dreary and desolate than that which awaited us, the outward-bound, in the early morning of the 20th of last December. The same sullen neutral tint pervaded and possessed everything—the leaden sky—the bleak brown shores over against us—the dull grey stonework lining the quays—the foul yellow water—shading one into the other, till the division-lines became hard to discern. Even where the fierce gust swept off the crests of the river wavelets, boiling and breaking angrily, there was scant contrast of colour in the dusky spray, or murky foam.

The chafing Mersey tried in vain to make himself heard. Other sounds—a voice, for instance, two yards from your ear—were drowned by the trumpet of the strong north-wester. All through the past night,

B

we listened to that note of war; we could feel the
railway carriages trembling and quivering, as if
shaken by some rude giant's hand, when they halted
at any exposed station; and, this morning, the pilots
shake their wise, grizzled heads, and hint at worse
weather yet in the offing. For forty-eight hours
the storm-signals had never been lowered, nor
changed, except to intimate the shifting of a point
or two in the current of the gale, and few vessels, if
any, had been found rash enough to slight the
Admiral's warning.

It had been gravely discussed, we heard afterwards,
by the owners and captain of the Asia, whether she
should venture to sea that day; finally, the question
was left to the latter to decide. There are as nice
points of honour, and as much jealous regard for
professional credit in the merchant service as in any
other; only once, since the line was started, has a
'Cunarder' been kept in port by wind or weather;
this was the commander's first trip across the
Atlantic since his promotion: you may guess which
way the balance turned.

We waited on the landing-stage, one long cold hour.
That huge square structure, ordinarily steady and
solid as the mainland itself, was pitching and rolling,
not much less lively than a Dutch galliot in a
sea-way; and the tug that was to take us on board,
parted three hawsers before she could make fast
alongside. It was hard to keep one's footing on

the shaking, slippery bridge; but in ten minutes all staggered or tumbled, as choice or chance directed, on to the deck of the little steamer. I was looking for a dry corner, when an American passenger made room for me very courteously, and I began to talk to him—about the weather, of course. He had a keen, intellectual face, pleasant withal, and kindly, and in its habitual expression not devoid of genial humour. But, at that moment, it was possessed by an unutterable misery. No wonder.

"I was ill the whole way over from America," he said, "and *then* we started with bright weather, and a fair wind."

I was much attracted by the voice, betraying scarcely any Transatlantic accent: it was quiet and calm in tone, like that of a brave man on his way to encounter some irresistible pain or woe, but saddened by an agony of anticipation: he presaged, only too truly, 'the burden of the atmosphere and the wrath to come.'

Another struggle and scramble—and we are on board, at last. It is some comfort to exchange that wretched little wet tug for the deck of the Asia; though a trifle unsteady even now, she oscillates after the sober and stately fashion befitting a mighty 'liner.' Half an hour sees the end of the long stream of mail-bags, and the huge bales of newspapers shipped: then the moorings are cast loose; there rises the faintest echo of a cheer—who could

be enthusiastic on such a morning?—the vast wheels
turn slowly and sullenly, as if hating the hard work
before them; and we are fairly off.

The waves and weather grew rapidly wilder as we
neared blue water: just after passing the light-ship, we
saw a large vessel driving helplessly and—the sailors
said—hopelessly, among the breakers of the North
Sands.   She had tried to run in without a pilot, and
ours seemed to think her fate the justest of judg-
ments; but to disinterested and unprofessional spec-
tators the sight was very sad, and somewhat dis-
couraging.   So, with omen and augury, as well as
the wind, dead against us,

The Sword went out to sea.

All that day and night the Asia staggered and
weltered on through the yeasty Channel waves, breaking in her passengers, rather roughly, for a conflict
with vaster billows.   Thirteen hours of hard steaming
barely brought us abreast of Holyhead.   The gale
moderated towards morning, and we ran along the
Irish coast under a blue sky, making Queenstown
shortly after sundown.

By this time I had become acquainted with my
cabin-mate, in which respect I was singularly fortunate.   M. —— was a thorough Parisian, and a
favourable specimen of his class.   Small of stature,
and slender of proportion—a very important point
where space is so limited—low-voiced, and sparing

of violent expletives or gestures, delicately neat in
his person and apparel—one could hardly have
selected a more amiable colleague. Under circumstances of some difficulty, I can aver that he conducted himself always with a perfect modesty and
decorum: he would preserve his equilibrium miraculously, when his perpendicular had been lost long
ago: he never fell upon me but once (sleeping on a
sofa, I was exposed defencelessly to all such contingencies), and then, lightly as thistle-down. On the
rare occasions when the *mal-de-mer* proved too much
for his valiant self-assertion, he yielded to an over-
ruling fate without groan or complaint; folding the
scanty coverlet around him, he would subside
gradually into his berth, composing his little limbs
with Cæsarean grace. His courtesy was invincible
and untiring; he was anxious to defer and conform
even to my insular prejudices. Discovering that I
was in the habit of daily immersion in cold water—
a feat not to be accomplished without much toil,
trouble, and abrasion of the cuticle—he thought it
necessary to simulate a like performance, though
nothing would have tempted him to incur such needless danger. His endeavours to mislead me on this
point, without actually committing himself, were
ingenious and wily in the extreme. Sitting in the
saloon, at the most incongruous hours of day and
night, he would exclaim—" J'ai l'idée, de prendre
bientôt mon bain"—or he would speak, with a remi-

niscent shiver, of an imaginary plunge taken that
morning. I don't think I should ever have been
deluded, even if my curiosity had not led me to
question the steward; but never, by word or look,
did I impugn the reality of that Barmecide bath.
To his other accomplishments, M. ——— added a very
pretty talent for piquet; the match was even enough,
though, to be interesting, at almost nominal stakes,
and so we got pleasantly through many hours—dark,
wet, or boisterous.

We were not a numerous company—only thirty-
three in all: few amateurs travel at this inclement
season. I knew only one other Englishman on board,
an officer in the Rifle Brigade, returning to Canada
from sick leave. Among the Americans, was Cyrus
Field, the energetic promoter of the Atlantic Telegraph, then making (I think he said) his thirtieth
transit within five years. He was certainly entitled
to the freedom of the Ocean, if intimate acquaintance
with every fathom of its depth and breadth could
establish a claim: it rather surprised me, afterwards, to see such science and experience yield
so easily to the common weakness of seafaring
humanity. Mr. Field told me that, throughout the fearful weather to which the Niagara and
Agamemnon were exposed on their first attempt to
lay down the cable, he never once felt a sensation of
nausea; the body had not time to suffer till the mind
was relieved from its strain.

For three days after leaving Queenstown, the west winds met us, steady and strong; but it was not till the afternoon of Christmas-day, that the sea began to rise in earnest, and the weather to portend a gale. Then, the Atlantic seemed determined to prove that report had not exaggerated the inclemency of a winter passage. It blew harder and harder all Friday, and after a brief lull on Saturday—as though gathering breath for the final onset—the storm fairly reached its height, and then slowly abated, leaving us substantial tokens of its visit, in the shape of shattered boats, and the ruin of all our port bulwarks forward of the deck-house. I fancy there was nothing extraordinary in the tempest, and, in a stout ship, with plenty of sea-room, there is probably little real danger; but, about the intense discomfort, there could be no question. I speak with no undue bitterness, for of nausea, in any shape, I know little or nothing, but—oh, mine enemy!—if I could feel certain you were well out in the Atlantic, experiencing for just one week the weather that fell to our lot, I would abate much of my animosity, purely from satiation of revenge.

Unless absolutely prostrated by illness, the voyager of course has a ravenous appetite; such being the case, what can be more exasperating than having to grapple with a sort of dioramic dinner, where the dishes represent a series of dissolving views,— mutton and beef, of mature age, leaping about with

a playfulness only becoming living lambs or calves—
while the proverb of 'cup and lip' becomes a truism
from perpetual illustration ?   Neither is it agreeable,
after falling into an uncertain doze, to feel dampness
mingling strangely with your dreams, and to awake
to find yourself, as it were, an island in a little Salt
Lake formed by distillation through invisible crevices.

> Laith, laith were our gude Scot lords
> To wet their cork-heeled shoon,

says the grand old ballad; so, I suppose, it is not
' unbecoming the character of an officer and a gentleman ' to hold such midnight irrigation in utter ab-
horrence.

On one of these occasions, I abandoned a post no
longer tenable, and went into the small saloon
close by, to seek a dry spot whereon to finish the
night. I found it occupied by a ghastly man, with
long, wild grey hair, and a white face—striding
staggeringly up and down—moaning to himself in a
harsh, hollow voice—" No rest. I can't rest." He
never spoke any other words, and never ceased repeating these, while I remained to hear him. Instantly,
there came back to my memory a horrible German
tale—read and forgotten fifteen years ago—of a certain
old and unjust steward, Daniel by name, who, having
murdered his master by casting him down an
oubliette, ever haunted the fatal tower—first as a
sleep-walker, then as a restless ghost—moaning and

gibbering to himself, and tearing at a walled-up door
with bleeding hands. The train of thought thereby
suggested was so very sombre, that I preferred
returning to my cabin, and climbing into an un-
furnished berth, to spending more minutes in that
weird company. I never made the man out satisfactorily afterwards. It is possible that he was one
of the few who scarcely showed on deck till we were
in sight of land ; but rather, I believe, like other
visions and voices of the Night, he changed, past recognition, under the garish light of day.

Then come the noisy nuisances, extending through
all the diapason of sound. One—the most annoying
—to which the ear never becomes callous by use, is
the incessant wash, not only alongside, but overhead.
At intervals—more frequent, of course, after our
bulwarks were swept away—the green water came
tumbling on board by tons ; and, being unable to
escape quickly enough by the after-scuppers, surged
backwards and forwards with every roll of the vessel,
as if it meant to keep you down, and bury you for
ever. Lying in my berth, I could feel the heavy seas
smite the strong ship one cruel blow after another on
her bows or beam, till, at last, she would seem to stop
altogether, and, dropping her head, like a glutton in
the P.R., would take her punishment sullenly, without an effort at rising or resistance. Nevertheless, I
stand by the Asia as a right good boat for rough
weather, though she is not a flyer, and sometimes

could hardly do more than hold her own. Eighty-
one knots in the twenty-four hours, was all the
encouragement the log could give, one day.

I liked our commander exceedingly. He had just
left the Mediterranean station, and there still abode
with him a certain languid Levantine softness of voice
and manner: when he came in to dinner, out of the
wild weather, the moral contrast with the turmoil
outside was quite refreshing. Report speaks highly
of Captain Grace's seamanship; I believe in him
far more implicitly than in one of those hoarse and
blusterous Tritons, who think roughness and readiness inseparable, and talk to you as if they were
hailing a consort.

The library on board was not extensive, consisting
(with the exception of 'The Newcomes,') chiefly of
religious works of the Nonconformist school, and
tales which have long ago passed into surplus stock,
or been withdrawn from general circulation. But
there was one invaluable novel, which I shall always
remember gratefully. I never got quite through it;
but read enough to be enabled to affirm that its
principles are unexceptionable, its style grammatically
faultless, and its Purpose sustained (ah, how pitilessly!)
from first to last : the few amatory scenes are conducted with the most rigid propriety ; and when there
occurs a lovers'-quarrel, the contending parties hurl
high moral truths at each other, instead of idle re-
proaches. But it is mainly as a soporific that I

would recommend 'Silwood:' on four different occasions, under most trying circumstances, it succeeded perfectly and promptly with me, for which relief— unintentional, perchance—I render much thanks to the unknown author, and wish 'more power to his arm.'

Quite crippled for the time being by rheumatism, I was in bad form for clambering about the sloping, slippery planks; nevertheless I did contrive to crawl up to the hurricane-deck just before sun-down, about the crisis of the gale. I confess to being disappointed in the 'rollers': it may be, that their vast breadth and volume takes off from their apparent height; but I scarcely thought it reached Dr. Scoresby's standard —from 25 to 30 feet, if I remember right, from trough to crest. One realises thoroughly the abysmal character of the turbulent chaos; and there is a sensation of infiniteness around and below you, not devoid of grandeur; but, as an exhibition of the puissance of angry water, I do not think the mid-ocean tempest equal to the storm which brings the thunder of the surf full on the granite bulwarks of Western Ireland.

It must be owned, that the conversational resources of our small society were limited. Very often, some selfishness mingled with my sincere compassion for the prostrated sufferings of my Philadelphian friend of the tug-boat; for, whenever his weary aching head would allow of the exertion, he could talk on almost any subject, fluently and well. He was returning from a long visit to Paris, and a rapid tour through Germany and Southern Europe. Most of the countries that he had been compelled to hurry over, I had loitered through in days past; I ought to have been shamed by the contrast in our recollections —his, so clear and systematical—mine, so vague and dim. An intellectual American, travelling through strange lands, does certainly look at nature, animate and inanimate, after the practical business-like fashion peculiar to his race; but it would be unfair to infer that such minds are necessarily unappreciative. At all events, the concentrative synthetical power, that takes in surrounding objects at a single glance, and retains them in a tolerably distinct classification, is rather enviable, even as a mental accomplishment.

We did not speak much about the troubles beyond sea, and the Philadelphian was somewhat reserved as to his proclivities. My impression is, that his sympathy tended rather Southward (all his early life had been spent in Alabama), but he declined to commit himself much, nor do I believe that he was a violent partisan either way. On one point he was very decided: Falkland himself could not have wished more devoutly for the termination of the Civil War—fatal, he said, to the interests, present and future, of both the combatant powers—ruinous to every class, with two exceptions; the adventurers who, having little to lose, gained, by joining the ranks of either army, a social position to which they could not otherwise have aspired ; and the speculators, who, directly or indirectly, fairly or unfairly, made gains, vast and unholy, such as wreckers are wont to gather in time of tempest and general disaster. He scarcely alluded to the corruption and peculation prevalent in high places, diluted in its downward percolation till sutlers and horse-thieves would strive in vain to emulate the fraudulent audacity of their superiors : it was well he spared me then, for soon after landing my eyes and ears grew weary with the repetition of these ignoble details. To illustrate how heavily the taxes were already beginning to weigh on the non-militant population, my informant proved to me, by very clear figures, that, if he individually could secure permanent exemption from such burdens, by the absolute sacrifice of one tenth of his whole property, real and personal, the commutation would be decidedly advantageous to him. True, he represented a class whose incomes exceeded a certain standard, and therefore suffered rather more heavily ; but the same calculation, with very slight alterations, applied to all other subordinate ones.

Grave and mild of speech was that Philadelphian philosopher, without a trace of dogmatism or self-assertion in his tone ; nevertheless, I judged him to be a man of mark somewhere, and I afterwards heard that, albeit not a prominent politician, he had great honour in his own country.

Strong head-winds and a heavy sea baffled us till

we had cleared the longitude of Cape Race; then the weather softened, the breeze veered round till it blew on our quarter, and we had clear sky above us all the way in.   We sighted the first pilot-boat on the afternoon of January 3rd, and, as she came sweeping down athwart us, with her broad white wings full spread, our glasses soon made out the winning number of the sweepstakes, " 22." The dinner-hour was long past when the beautiful little schooner rounded to, under our lee; but all appetite just then was merged in a craving for latest intelligence.

It was a caricaturist's study—the crowd of keen, anxious faces round the gangway, as the pilot came aboard.   He was a stout man, of agricultural exterior, looking as if he were in the habit of ploughing anything rather than the deep sea; but it is the fashion of his guild to eschew the nautical as much as possible in their attire.   The 'anxious inquirers' got little satisfaction from him—he seemed taciturn of nature, or sullen—and they came back to where the rest of us stood on the hurricane deck, muttering discontentedly, " Gold at 46.   No news." It seemed very odd—such a complete stagnation of affairs military and civil—but we fed, in spite of disappointment. Before we rose from table, the truth began to ooze out.   One or two New York papers, that had slipped on board with the pilot, were more communicative than he would or could be.

Thousands of corpses, the full tale of which will

never be known till the Day of Judgment, lying rolled
in blood, with a handful of earth raked over them,
under the fatal Fredericksburg heights; the finest
army in Federaldom hurled back upon its entrench-
ments, nothing but darkness covering a disastrous, if
not shameful defeat; the papers crowded with dreary
funeral notices, showing how, to every great city of
the North, from hospital and battle-ground, the slain
are being gathered in, to be buried among their
own people; a wail of widows and orphans and
mothers, from homestead, hamlet, and town, over-
powering with its simple energy the bombastic war-
notes and false stage-thunder of the Press; rumours
of terrible battle in the far West, where, after three
days' hard fighting, Rosecrans barely holds his own;
and yet—" *No news!* "

It is an excellent quality in a soldier not to know
when he is beaten, but whether blind obstinacy will
succeed when it influences the rulers and destinies of
a great nation, is more than questionable. Pondering
these things, I remembered how, four thousand years
ago, a stiff-necked generation were brought to their
senses and on their knees: it was on the morning
after the visit of the Dark Angel, when Egypt awoke,
and found not a house in which there was not one
dead. If such fearful waste of life goes on here,
with no decisive or final advantage on either side
attained, that ancient curse may not be long in
recurring.

I rose, when the sun ought to have risen, on the following morning, intending to admire the famous harbour which Americans love to compare with the Neapolitan Bay. But long before we reached the Narrows,

> A blinding mist came up and hid the land
> As far as eye could see.

Very soon we were buried in fog, dense and Cimmerian as ever brooded over our own Thames or the Righi panorama. More and more slowly the paddles turned, till they stopped altogether ; it was dangerous to advance, ever so cautiously, when the keenest sight could not pierce half a ship's length ahead. So, there we lay at anchor for weary hours, listening to the church-bells chiming drowsily through the heavy air, till an enterprising tug ventured out for the mails, and sent another for the relief of the passengers.

The custom-house officers were not troublesome, and I was soon at the Brevoort House, the Parisian Pylades still faithfully following my fortunes. I was far from entreating him to leave me ; landing utterly alone in a strange land, one does not lightly cast aside companionship. For reasons easily understood, I had declined to avail myself of many proffered letters of introduction to New Yorkers.

That lonely feeling did not last long : the first object which caught my eye on the steps of the

Brevoort House was an honest English face—a face I have known and liked right well, these dozen years and more. There stood 'the Colonel' (any Ch. Ch. or Rifle Brigade man will recognise the *sobriquet*), beaming upon the world in general with the placid cheerfulness that no changes of time or place or fortune seem able to alter ; looking just as comfortable and thoroughly 'at home,' as he did, steering Horniblow to victory at Brixworth. I had heard that my old friend was on his way to England to join the Staff College, but had never reckoned on such a successful 'nick' as this. By my faith, the turns of luck beyond the Atlantic were not so frequent, as to excuse forgetfulness, when they did befall.

So I had aid and abetment in performing the little lionisation which is obligatory on a visitor to New York ; for the 'Colonel's' comrade, my fellow-voyager of the Asia, came to the same hotel.

Assisted by the Parisian, we made trial of the esculents peculiar to the country—gombo soup, sweet potatoes, terrapins, and canvas-backs—with much solemnity and satisfaction, agreeing, that fame had spoken truth for once, in extolling the two last-named delicacies. We went to the Opera, and there, in a brilliant *salle* of white and gold, spoilt, however, by the incongruity of bonnets mingling everywhere with full evening toilettes, assisted at a massacre— unmusical and melancholy—of ' Lucrezia.' We drove out through the crude, unfinished Central Park to

c

Harlem Lane, whither the trotters are wont to resort,
and saw several teams looking very much like work
(though no celebrities); almost all of the lean, rather
ragged form, which characterises, more or less, all
American-bred 'fast horses.' The ground was too
hard frozen to allow of anything beyond gentle exercise ; but, even at quarter-speed, that wonderful
hind-action was very remarkable. Watching those
clean, sinewy pasterns shoot forward—well *outside* of
the fore hoof-track—straight and swift as Mace's arm
in an 'upper-cut,' you marvel no longer at the mile-
time which hitherto has seemed barely credible.

Perhaps this same bitter weather may account for
our disappointment in the brilliancy of Broadway.
Several careful reviews of the sunny side, failed to
detect anything dangerously attractive in beauty,
equipage, or attire. It is probable, that most of the
lionnes had laid them down in their delicate dens,
waiting for a more clement season to renew external
depredations ; though sometimes you could just catch
a glimpse of bright eyes and a little pink nose peer-
ing over dark fur wrappings, as a brougham or
barouche, carefully closed, swept quickly by. We
visited Barnum, of course. I think a conversational
and communicative Albino was the most note-worthy
curiosity in the Museum, chiefly, from his intense
appreciation of the imposture of the whole concern
originated and directed by the King of Humbugdom.

The sanguine popular mind was unusually depressed

just then. The President's emancipatory proclamation had recently been issued, and seemed to adapt itself, with wonderful elasticity, to the discontents of all parties; not comprehensive enough for the ultra-Abolitionists, it was stigmatised by the Democrats as unconstitutional and oppressive; while moderate politicians agreed that, beyond irritating feelings already bitter enough, it would be practically invalid as an offensive measure. We shall see, hereafter, how these prognostications were justified.

But the first word in all men's mouths, for a day or two, at least, after my arrival, was—Monitor. That same gale which had buffeted the Asia so rudely on the high seas, had raged yet more savagely shorewards: the Merrimac's antagonist, like a drowning paladin of the mail-clad days, had sunk under her mighty armour, and now, with half her crew in their iron coffin, lay at rest in the crowded burial-ground on which Cape Hatteras looks down. Great discouragement and consternation—greater than has often been caused by the loss of any single vessel—fell upon all the North when the news came in. Ever since her famous duel, which the Federals never would allow was a drawn battle, they had elevated the Monitor into a national champion, and prophesied weeping in the South, if she and their batteries should meet: few, then, dared to insinuate a doubt about Charleston's certain fall, when once the leaguer was fairly mustered for assault.

c 2

Grave doubts were now expressed as to the sea-worthiness of all the new iron-clads, though their advocates could point to a sister of the unhappy Monitor, which had survived a great part of the same storm. That they all must be more unsafe in really rough weather than the crankiest of our old ' coffin-brigs,' seems quite ascertained now : the fact of their being unable to make headway through a heavy sea, unless towed by a consort, speaks for itself. The immediate cause of the Monitor's foundering (according to Captain Worden's account, which my informant had from his own lips) was a leak sprung, where her protruding stern-armour, coming down flat on the waves with every plunge of the vessel, became loosened from the main hull ; but, for some time before this was discovered, she seems to have spent more minutes under than above water, and nothing alive could have stood, unlashed, for a second on her deck. So great was the public disappointment, that the tribe of false prophets, whose cry of ' Go up to Ramoth-Gilead and prosper,' —usually not less loud in defeat than in success—deafens us here, did for awhile abate their blatancy ; while Ericsson—most confident of projectors—spake softly, below his breath, as he suggested faint excuse and encouragement.

The news from the West—hourly improving, and more clearly confirmed—were hardly welcomed as they deserved, and scarcely counter-balanced the naval disaster. It was not long, however, before

Rosecrans the Invincible came in for his full share of credit—perhaps not more than he merited. Few other Federal commanders can claim that epithet; and, though some people persisted in considering Murfreesburgh a Pyrrhic victory, it is certain that he held his ground manfully, and eventually advanced, where defeat, or even a retrograde movement, would have been simply ruin.

On the fifth day our small company were scattered —each going his own way, east, north, and south— while the Parisian abode still in New York.

CHAPTER II.

OF two lines to Philadelphia, I selected the longest, wishing to see the harbour, down which a steamer takes passengers as far as Amboy; but the Powers of the Air were unpropitious again; it never ceased snowing, from the moment we went on board a very unpleasant substitute for the regular passage-boat, till we landed on the railway pier. My first experience of American travel was not attractive. The crazy old craft puffed and snorted furiously, but failed to persuade any one that she was doing eight miles an hour; the grime of many years lay thick on her dusky timbers—dust under cover, and mud where the wet swept in,—while her close dark cabins were stifling enough to make you, after five minutes of vapour-bathing, plunge eagerly into the bitter weather outside. Indeed, there was not much to see, for the track lies on the inner and uglier side of Staten Island. The last few miles lead through marshes, with nothing taller growing than reeds and osiers.

For an hour or so after leaving Amboy, you look out on a country thickly populated, well cultivated, and trimly fenced, bearing a strong resemblance to parts of our own Eastern counties. We passed through one wood, in height of trees, sweep of ground, colour of soil, and build of boundary-fence so exactly like a certain cover in Norfolk similarly bisected by the rail, that I could have picked out the precise spot where, many a time and oft, I have waited for the 'rocketers.' But the character of the landscape soon changed ; loose sprawling ' zigzags,' or snake-fences, usurped the place of neat squared post-and-rails ; the stunted wood-land stretched farther afield, with rarer breaks of clearing; and the low hill-ranges, behind which the watery sun soon absconded, looked drearily bare in the distance.

It was pleasant, from the ferry-boat, which was our last change, to meet the lights of Philadelphia gleaming out on the broad dark Susquehanna.

I can say little of that staid, opulent, intensely respectable city — not even if the imputation of dullness, cast upon her by the more mercurial South, be a slander; for the few hours of my stay there were spent almost entirely with my Asiatic friend, whose invitations and inducements to a longer sojourn were very hard to resist. But I was impatient to get on (as men will be who cannot see their arm's-length into the future), and, at midnight, started again for Washington.

My recollections of that journey are the reverse of roseate. The atmosphere of the cars—windows her-

metic, and stoves red-hot—made one look back
regretfully on the milder *inferno* of the passage-boat ;
the acrid apple-odour was more pungently nau-
seating ; and the abomination of expectoration less
carefully dissembled.   Besides this, I was afflicted by
another nuisance, purely private and personal.

Whether there be any such thing as love at first
sight or no, is a question—grave or gay, as you choose
to discuss it—but, that instinctive antipathies exist, is
most certain.   I was the victim of one of such that
night.   Waiting for change in the ticket-office, my
eye lighted on a dark man, of African appearance,
standing unpleasantly near; and, for a second or two, I
could not get rid of a horrible fascination, compelling
me to stare.   I say ' dark man ' advisedly, for it
would have been hard to guess at his original colour,
unless his cast of feature had given a line.   Now,
I have seen Irish squatters in their cabins, London
outcasts in their penny lodgings, and beggars of
Southern Europe in their nameless dens ; but the conviction flashed upon me (and it has never since passed
away), that I was then gazing on a dirtier specimen of
healthy humanity than I had ever yet foregathered
with.   I believe that, all the rains of heaven beating on
his brow would not have altered its dinginess by a
shade, nor penetrated one of the earthy layers that had
thickened there ; a thunder-shower must have glanced
off, as water will do from tough, hardened clay. Rough
patches of hair, scanty and straggling, like the vegeta-

tion of waste, barren lands, grew all over his cheeks and chin (a negro with an ample, honest beard is an anomaly); and a huge bush of wool—unkempt, I dare swear, from earliest infancy—seemed to repel the ruins of a nondescript hat. Whether he was really uglier than his fellows I cannot remember—I was so absorbed in contemplating and realising his surpassing squalor—but the expression of the uncouth face (if it had any whatsoever) was, I think, neither ferocious nor sullen. There is generally a ' coloured car ' attached to every train; for you will find the tender-hearted Abolitionist, in despite of his African sympathies, when it is a question of personal contact or association, quite as earnest in keeping those ' innocent blacknesses ' aloof, as the haughtiest Southerner. On the present occasion there was no such distinction of races. I do not think the contraband was conscious of the effect produced by his laidly presence; it was probably simple accident which brought him so often in my neighbourhood ; but, wherever I moved through the crowded cars, seeking for a seat, the loose shambling limbs and dull vacant eyes seemed impelled to follow. At last I lost my *béte noire,* and found a place close to the door, with nothing but a low pile of logs in my front. I was tired, and soon began to doze ; but I woke up with a start and a shudder, as a haunted man might do, becoming aware, in sleep, of the approach of some horrible thing. There He sat, on the logs close to my feet, in a heavy stertorous slumber; his huge head rocking to and fro, and his features hideously contorted, as he growled and gibbered to himself in an unknown tongue, like some dreaming Caliban. I arose, and fled away swiftly from the face of my ' brother,' and, finding no other available resting-place, did battle on the outside platform with the keen night-wind.

I am indebted, however, to that honest contraband for a curious sight, which I should otherwise have missed—the crossing of the Gunpowder River. There, the train rushes, on a single track, over three-quarters of a mile of tremulous trestlework, without an apology for a side-rail, so that you look straight down into the dark water, over which you seem wafted with no visible support beneath. The effect is sufficiently startling, especially when it is seen as I saw it, under a bright, capricious moon. From Baltimore, the cars were less crowded, and I encountered my dusky tormentor no more.

If there is much in first impressions, I was not likely to be enchanted with Washington.

The snow, just then beginning to melt, lay inches deep on the half-frozen soil; everything looked unnaturally and unutterably dreary in the bleak leaden dawn-light; and, as I drove down Pennsylvania Avenue (after rejection at the lodgings to which I had been recommended), the first object that caught my eye was a huge placard :—

EMBALMING OF THE DEAD.

These ghastly advertisements are not unfrequent in that part of the city, and I was informed that the trade occasionally does a very brisk business.

After waiting for two hours in the hall of the Metropolitan, like a client in some patrician ante-chamber, they *did* accord me a tolerable room on the sublimest story.

I called that same afternoon on Lord Lyons, to whom I brought an introductory letter. I have to thank the British Legation for much courteous kindness, and for two very pleasant evenings, on the first of which I was the guest of the Chief, on the second, of his secretaries. Here will (if I ever leave it behind me) begin and end my agreeable reminiscences of Washington. I disliked it cordially at first sight; I was thoroughly bored before I had got through my stay of seventy hours; I utterly abominate and execrate the city,

From turret to foundation-stone,

at this moment, as I catch a narrow glimpse of its outskirts through the rusty window-bars of the Old Capitol. Should the southern Mazeppas, whose banners have already floated in sight of Arlington Heights, ever work their will here, I could name one Briton, whose composure will not be ruffled by compassion at hearing the news. If there is anything in presentiments, surely one of these, thus early in my pilgrimage, whispered warnings to me, though I was deafer than the adder just then.

There was in Washington, of course, the usual
crowd—official, political, and mercantile,—with a
vast supplement of hangers-on and aspirants, that
always follows the meeting of Congress ; and, besides,
the influx never ceased of all officers who could
get leave—of many who could not—from the army of
the Potomac. Speaking impartially—for I scarcely
interchanged four words with an American during
my stay—I thought the military element the most
repulsive.

It would be unfair to cavil at the absence of a
martial bearing in men, who, having followed other
professions all their lives, so lately and suddenly took
up that of arms. In this singular war, whole regiments have been sent into action (as at Antietam)
without even an hour's practice in file-firing, and
have stood their ground, too, manfully, though helplessly, the merest food for cannon. So it is not strange,
if the lawyers, merchants, clerks, stock-brokers, bar-
keepers, and newspaper-editors, who officer the volun-
teer-corps, should laugh 'setting-up' preliminaries
to scorn, and consider a few days of rough battalion-
drill, a satisfactory qualification for efficient service in
the field.

In spite of these disadvantages, it is indisputable
that the Yankee will fight right stubbornly, after his
own fashion, though rarely with the dash and fire of the
Southerner. Considering the raw and heterogeneous
materials out of which the huge armies of the North

have been formed, individual instances of personal cowardice are creditably rare. Even in the cases of disorderly retreats, I believe discipline, rather than pluck, to have been wanting. Martinets and formalists would certainly be out of place here, and some of the technicalities of the art of war may well be dispensed with ; nevertheless, all these palliations do not alter my unfavourable impression of the Federal officer on furlough.

Once out of the camp, and among familiar scenes again,—the recent centurion falls back, swiftly and easily, into the slovenly habits and careless demeanor that were natural to him before he was called to command ; his uniform begins to look like a masquerade-dress hired for the occasion ; of the hard and, perhaps, gallant service of months past, there is soon no other evidence, than an unnecessary loudness of speech, and a readiness to seize on any occasion to bluster or blaspheme. A friend of mine once remarked (by way of excuse for being detected in the most eccentric *déshabillé*) that ' the British dragoon, under *any* circumstances, was a respectable and elevating sight.' I do not think, the most amiable stranger would be inclined to concede as much to an officer of Federal volunteers, encountering that warrior in his native bar or oyster-saloon. On the whole, I prefer the real Zouave, *en tapageur*, to his Transatlantic imitator ; the former, at least swaggers,—professionally.

It would hardly be honest, to take the 'loafers' of Washington as fair representatives of their order: there are, no doubt, better—if not braver—soldiers in the front; and, perhaps, even the queer specimens then before me might look decent, if not dignified, under the earnest light of battle.

But, wherever I was brought in contact with portions of the Federal army (I never saw a whole regiment in review-order), I was forcibly struck, with the entire absence of the 'smartness' which distinguishes our own, and much of the Continental, soldiery. While I was at Washington, there were three squadrons of regular cavalry encamped in the centre of the city. These troops were especially on home-service — guard-mounting, orderly-duty, &c.— with no field or picket work whatever. There was no more excuse for slovenliness than might have been allowed to a regiment in huts, at Aldershott or Shorncliffe. I wish, the critical eye of the present Inspector General could light on that encampment; if he preserved his wonted courteous calmness, it would be a very Victory of Suffering: the effect upon his predecessor would be instantly fatal.

The arms looked tolerably clean and serviceable; but bridle-bits, bosses, spurs, and accoutrements were crusted with rust and grime; boots, buttons, and clothing were innocent of the brush, as the horses' coats of the curry-comb. The most careful grooming could not have made the generality of these animals look anything but ragged and weedy—rather dear at the Government price of 115—120 dollars,— and their housings were not calculated to set them off to advantage. The saddle — a modification of the Mexican principle of raw hide stretched over a wooden frame—carries little metal-work: it is lighter, I think, than ours, and more abruptly peaked, but not uncomfortable; being thrown well off the spine and withers, there is little danger of sore backs with ordinary care in settling the cloth or blanket. The heavy clog of wood and leather, closed in front, and only admitting the fore-part of the foot, which serves as a stirrup, is unsightly in the extreme : its advantages are said to be, protection from the weather, and the impossibility of the rider's entanglement; but the sole has no grip whatever, and, rising to give full effect to a sabre-cut, would be out of the question. Besides a halter, a single rein, attached to rather a clumsy bit, is the usual trooper's equipment: to this is attached the in-evitable ring-martingale, without which few Federal cavaliers, civil or military, would consider themselves safe.

I cannot conceive such an anomaly as a thorough Yankee *horseman*. Given—one, or a span of trotters, to be yoked after the neatest fashion, and to be driven gradually and scientifically up to top-speed—the Northerner is quite at home, and can give you a

wrinkle or two worth keeping. But the habit
of hauling at horses, which often go as much on the
bit as on the traces, is destructive to 'hands.' If
the late-lamented Assheton Smith were compelled to
witness the equitation here, he would suffer almost as
much, as Macaulay in the purgatory which Canon
Sydney imagined for the historian. I have discussed
that martingale-question with several good judges and
breeders of American blood-stock; but I never could get
them *quite* to agree in the absurdity, of tying down a
colt's head for the rest of his natural life, without
regard to his peculiar propensities—star-gazing, boring,
or neutral. The custom, of course, never could prevail where men were in the habit of crossing a
country; but an American horse is scarcely ever put
at anything beyond the ruins of a rail-fence, and
there are few, north of the Potomac, that I should
like to ride at four feet of stiff timber. It is very
different in the South, where many men from infancy
pass their out-door life in the saddle: from what I
have heard, Carolina, Louisiana, and Georgia—to say
nothing of the wild Texan rangers—could show riders
who, when the first strangeness had worn off, would
hold their own tolerably in England, over a fair hunting country, in any ordinary run.

On the outbreak of the war, volunteers enlisted in
the Federal cavalry, who—far from being able to
manage a horse—could not bridle one without assistance; and a conscript, who could keep his saddle,

through an entire day, without 'taking a voluntary,' was considered by his fellows as a credit to the regiment, and almost an accomplished dragoon. Such a thing as a military riding-school has, I believe, never been thought of, away from West Point; the drill is simply that of mounted infantry. Things are better now than they were; a Federal cavalryman can at least sit saddlefast, to receive and return a sabre-cut: there have been some sharp skirmishes of late, and, allowing for exaggeration, Averill's encounter with Fitzhugh Lee brought out real work on both sides.

Looking at that squalid encampment, it was easy to realise all one had heard of the mortality among the horses in the army of the Potomac, where no natural causes could justify it. Unless some sympathy exists between the two—unless the trooper takes some pride or interest in the animal he rides, beyond that of being conveyed safely from point to point—it is vain to expect that the comforts of the latter will be greatly cared for. General orders are powerless here, and the personal supervision of the officers—even if 'stables' were as carefully attended as in our own service—would only touch the surface of the evil. That utter absence of *esprit de corps* and soldierly self-respect has cost the Federal treasury many millions; nor will the drain ever cease till re-mounts shall be no more needed.

The foregoing remarks apply exclusively to the

D

tenue of the privates and non-commissioned officers ;
those of superior rank, that I met, were tolerably
correct, both in dress and equipment ; several, indeed, were mounted on really powerful chargers, and
rode them not amiss, though with a seat as unprofessional as can be conceived.

The military loungers monopolise all the leisure
of Washington—by day at least ; for, if all tales
are true, the legislators, in the evening and small
hours, are wont to unbend somewhat freely from their
labours ; and the Senate acts wisely, in not risking
through a night-session the little dignity it has left to
lose. But, with few exceptions, every civic face meets
you with the same anxious, worried look of unsatis-
fied craving ; there is hunger in all the restless, eager
eyes ; the thin, impatient lips work nervously, as
if scarcely able to repress the cry, which the Children
of the Horse-leech have uttered since the beginning
of time. It is easy to understand this, when you
remember that, at such a season, there gathers here—
besides the legion of politicians and partisans, and the
mighty army of contractors—a vaster host of persons
interested in the private bills submitted to Congress,
and of candidates for the numerous pieces of prefer-
ment which are being vacated and created daily.
Before the smallest of these has lain open for an hour,
there will be scores of shrill claimants wrangling over
it, summoned from the four winds of heaven by the
unerring instinct of the Rapacidæ.

Every one, of any official or political standing, can
either influence or dispose of a certain amount of
patronage; to such, life must sometimes be made a
heavy burden. Human nature shrinks from the con-
templation of what each successive President must
be doomed to undergo. His nerves ought to be of
iron, and his conscience of brass, or a Gold Coast
governorship might prove a less-dangerous dignity.
The character best fitted for the post would be such
an one as Gallio, the tranquil cynic of Antioch.

Marking and hearing these things, I thoroughly
appreciated an anecdote told me on board the Asia.
At Mobile, in 1849, the Philadelphian met President
Polk, then on his way home from Washington, his
term having just expired. He took up office—a
cheery, sanguine man, quite as healthy as the generality of his compatriots at forty-five; he laid it down
—a helpless invalid, shattered in body and mind,
past hope of revival. My informant, who knew him
well, was much shocked at the change, but tried to
console the Ex-President, by speaking of the important measures that made his administration one of
the most eventful since that of Washington; hinting,
that such grave responsibility, and continual excitement, might well account for exhaustion and reaction.
The sick man shook his head drearily, and put the
implied compliment aside; he was past such vanities
then.

"You're wrong," he said. "It isn't Oregon, or

Mexico, or Texas, but the office-hunters, that have brought me—where I am."

In that answer there was the simple solemnity, that attaches to the lightest words of the dying. Sixty days later, the speaker was 'sleeping down in Tennessee,'—never more to be vexed by the clamour of the cormorants, or waked by the clients keeping watch at his door. Nor was he a solitary victim. General Taylor did not live to see half his duty done, and the atmosphere of the White House, in one month, proved fatal to Harrison.

To a disinterested spectator—especially if he chance to be of indolent temperament—there is something very irritating in the ceaseless crowd, and hurry, and din. From early morning till long past midnight, you might search in vain, through any one of the principal hotels, for a quiet nook to write or read in, unless it were found in your own chamber, where the appliances of comfort are more than limited. All private sitting-rooms are instantly engaged at fabulous prices, and, in the public parlours, the feminine element reigns with no divided sway: it is difficult to appreciate even a newspaper 'leader,' with a prattle and titter around, wherein mingle tones, not *quite* so low and sweet as the voice of Cordelia. Those energetic civilians never seem at rest or at ease; they snatch their frequent drinks, upstanding and covered, as if they were just a minute behindhand for some appointment; bolting their food, as if dinner were a necessary medicinal evil.

Sooth to say, the edibles do not deserve much better treatment: the whole commissariat arrangements in the hotels is supremely uncomfortable. The guests feed separately; but no dinner can be served in the public rooms after five P.M. You can choose to any extent from a sufficiently ample, though very simple, *carte;* but your repast arrives *en masse*, no matter into how many courses it ought naturally to be divided, and is set down before you in un-covered dishes. Of course, when you arrive at the last, it retains scarcely a memory of the fire. I saw some of the *indigènes* obviate the inconvenience, by taking fish, flesh, and fowl on their plate at one and the same time, consuming the impromptu ' olla ' with a rapid, impartial voracity; but so bold an innovation on old-world customs would hardly suit a stranger. All liquors are rather higher in price and lower in quality than one would expect, consider-ing the place and season ; but the sum charged for unstinted board and a tolerable bed (from two to two and a half dollars per diem) is reasonable enough, especially during the present depreciation of the currency.

Out-door scenes were not much more attractive. The three-months' reign of Jupiter Pluvius, which has made this spring evilly notorious, had just begun in earnest. In the main avenues, on either side of

the rail-track of the cars, the mud was a trifle deeper
than that of a cross-lane, in winter, in the Warwick-
shire clays. To traverse the by-streets comfortably,
you require rather a clever animal over a country,
and especially good in 'dirt'; they are intersected
by frequent brooks, much wider and deeper than
that celebrated one which tested the prowess of *le
bonhomme* Briggs. There are rough stepping-
stones at some of the crossings, and the passage of
these, after nightfall, resembles greatly that of a
'shaking' bog, where the traveller has to leap from
tussock to moss-hag with agile audacity; the consequences of a false step being, in both cases, about the
same. I began to think regretfully of certain rugged
continental *pavés*, execrated in days gone by; they
at least had a firm bottom, more or less remote.

The public buildings of Washington do not
attempt architectural display: with scarcely an
exception, they are severely simple and square. But
there is a certain grandeur in the masses of white
marble, which is everywhere lavishly employed; the
Capitol stands right well—alone, on the crest of
a low, abrupt slope, with nothing to intercept the view
from its terraces, seaward, and up the valley of the
Potomac. The effect will probably be better when
wind and weather shall have slightly toned down
the sheen of the fresh-hewn stones, so dazzling, now,
as almost to tire the eye.

I lingered some time in the stranger-galleries of

Congress, but—'a plague on both their Houses'—
there was no question of stirring interest before
either. I had hoped to see at least one representative committed to the custody of the Sergeant-at-
Arms; but, on that day, the hardly-worked official
had rest from his labours. Only a few hours later,
an irascible senator (from Delaware, I think) created
a temporary excitement by defying, first his political
opponent, and then, generally, all powers that be;
eventually displaying the revolver, which is the *ratio
ultima* of so many Transatlantic debates. I heard
some 'tall talking,' enforced by much energy of
gesture and resonance of tone; but not a period
verging on eloquence. The speakers generally
seemed to have studied in the simple school of the
'stump' or the tavern, and, when at a loss for an
argument, would introduce a diatribe against the
South, or a declaration of fidelity to the Union,—very
much as they might have proposed a toast or sentiment,—supremely disregardful of such trifles as
relevancy or connection. The retort—more or less
courteous—seemed much favoured by these honest
rhetoricians, and appreciated by the galleries, who,
at such times, applauded sympathetically, in despite
of menace or intercession of Vice-President or
Speaker. Nobody, indeed, took much notice of
either of these two dignitaries; and they appeared
perfectly reconciled to their position. You would
not often find orators and audience understand one

another more thoroughly : the easy freedom of the
whole concern was quite festive in its informality.

Having secured a portion of my English letters
(one or more were retained for the recreation and,
I hope, improvement of the post-official mind),
nothing detained me in Washington beyond the
fourth morning. I turned northwards the more
cheerfully, because it involved escape from a certain
chamber-maiden to whose authority I was subjected at the Metropolitan—the most austere tyrant
that ever oppressed a traveller. That grim White
Woman might have paired with the Ancient Mariner
—she was so deep-voiced, and gaunt, and wan. On
the few occasions when I ventured to summon her,
she would 'hold me with her glittering eye' till I
quailed visibly beneath it, utterly scorning and reject-
ing some mild attempts at conciliation. I am certain,
she suspected me of meditating some black private
or public treachery ; and I know, there was joy in
her granite heart when circumstances brought me, at
last, in my innocence, before the bar of her offended
country. On that fourth morning, however, the
mood of Sycorax seemed to change ; there was a
ghastly gaiety in her manner, and on her rigid lips
an Homeric smile more terrible than a frown. Then
I pondered within myself—" If her hate be heavy to
bear, what—what—would her love be ?" The unutterable horror of the idea gave me courage, that I
might otherwise have lacked, to confess my intentions

of absconding. But I avow that the liberality of the parting largesse is to be attributed to the meanest motives of personal fear.

On the railway platform, shaking the mud of Washington from my drenched boots, I purposed never to return thither. But I reckoned without my future hosts, MM. Seward and Stanton, who, though I have trespassed on their hospitality, now for some weeks, seem still loth to let me go.

CHAPTER III.

CAPUA.

THE southward approach to Baltimore is very well managed. The railroad makes an abrupt curve, as it sweeps round the marshy woodlands through which the Patapsco opens out into its estuary; so that you have a fair view of the entire city, swelling always upwards from the water's edge, on a cluster of low, irregular hills, to the summit of Mount Vernon. From that highest point soars skyward a white, glistening pillar, crowned by Washington's statue. I have seldom seen a monument better placed, and it is worthy of its advantages. The figure retains much of the strength and grace for which in life it was renowned; if ever features were created worthy of the deftest sculptor and the purest marble, such, surely, was the birthright of that noble, serene face.

No one, that has sojourned in Washington, can be ten minutes in Baltimore without being aware of a great and refreshing change. You leave the hurry and bustle of traffic behind at the railway station, and are never subjected to such nuisances till you return thither. Even in the exclusively commercial squares of

the city there reigns comparative leisure, for, except
in the establishments of government contractors, or
others directly connected with the supply of the army
business is by no means brisk just now. You may
pass through Baltimore Street, the main artery bisect-
ing the town from east to west, at any hour, without
encountering a denser or busier throng than you
would meet in Regent Street, any afternoon *out* of
the season ; and, about the usual promenade-time, the
proportion of fair *flâneuses* to the meaner masculine
herd would be nearly the same.

I betook myself to Guy's Hotel, which had been
recommended to me as quiet and comfortable : for
many people it would have been *too* quiet. The black
waiters carried the science of 'taking things easy' to
a rare perfection ; they were thoroughly polite and
even kindly in manner, and never dreamed of
objecting to any practicable order, but—as for carrying it out within any specified time—*altra cosa.*
After a few vain attempts and futile remonstrances,
a philosophical guest would recognise, resignedly,
the absolute impossibility of obtaining breakfast,
however simple, under forty-five minutes from the
moment of commanding the same ; indeed that was
very good time ; I positively aver that I have waited
longer for eggs, tea, and toast. I never tried abuse
or reproach ; for I chanced, early in my stay, to
be present, when an impatient traveller voided the
vials of his wrath on the head of the chief attendant;

insisting, with many strange oaths, on his right to obtain cooked food, of some sort, within the half-hour.

Years ago, I was amused, at the *Gaietés*, by a common-place scene enough of stage-temptation. *Madelon*, driven into her last intrenchments by the sophistries of the wily aristocrat, objected timidly, " *Mais, Monseigneur, j'aime mon mari.*" For a moment the *Marquis* was surprised, and seemed to reflect. Then he said, " *Tiens, tu aimes ton mari? C'est bizarre: mais—après tout—ce n'est pas defendu.*" As he spoke, he smiled upon his simple vassal—evidently wavering between amusement and compassion.

With just such a smile—allowing for the exaggeration of the African physiognomy—did 'Leonard' contemplate his victim, and me, the bystander; and then—sauntered slowly from the room, without uttering one word. It was a great moral lesson, and I profited by it. But, in truth, there was little to complain of; the quarters were clean and comfortable, and one got, in time, as much as any reasonable man could desire. The arrangements are on the European system, *i.e.*, there are no fixed hours for meals, which are ordered from the *carte*, and no fixed charge for board. I should have remained there permanently, had it not been for one objection, which eventually overcame my aversion to change. The basement story of the house was occupied by a bar and oyster saloon; the pungent testaceous odours, mounting from those lower regions, gave the offended nostrils no respite or rest;

in a few minutes, a robust appetite, albeit watered by
cunning bitters, would wither, like a flower in the
fume of sulphur. Half-a-dozen before dinner have
always satiated my own desire for these molluscs;
before many days were over, I utterly abominated
the name of the species; familiarity only made the
nuisance more intolerable, and I fled at last,—fairly
ostracised. How the *habitués* stood it, was a mystery,
till I recognised the fact, that there is no accident of
pleasure or pain to which humanity is liable, no antecedent of rest or exertion, no untimeliness of hour
or incongruity of place, which will render an apple
or an oyster inopportune to the American *bour-
geois.*

My first visit in Baltimore was to the British
Consul, to whom I brought credentials from a member of the Washington Legation. I shall not easily
forget the many courtesies, for which I have never
adequately thanked Mr. Bernal: few English travellers leave Baltimore, without carrying away grateful recollections of his pleasant house in Franklin
Street, and without having received some kindness,
social or substantial, from the fair hands which dispense its hospitalities, so gently and gracefully.

On that same evening my name was entered as
an honorary member of the Maryland Club. It
would be absurd to compare this institution with the
palaces of our own metropolis; but, in all respects,
it may fairly rank with the best class of yacht-clubs.

You find there, besides the ordinary writing and reading accommodation, a pleasant lounge from early afternoon to early morning; a fair French cook, pitilessly monotonous in his *carte;* a good steady rubber at limited points; and a perfect billiard-room. In this last apartment it is well worth while to linger, sometimes, for half an hour, to watch the play, if the ' Chief' chances to be there. I have never seen an amateur to compare with this great artist, for certainty and power of cue: a short time before my arrival, at the cannon game, on a table without pockets, he scored 1015 on one break.

I went through many introductions that evening; and, in the next fortnight, received ample and daily proofs of the proverbial hospitality of Baltimore. There are residents—praisers of the time gone by—who cease not to lament the convivial decadence of the city; but such deficiency is by no means apparent to a stranger.

If *gourmandise* be the favourite failing in these parts, there is surely some excuse for the sinners. Probably no one tract on earth, of the same extent, can boast of so many delicacies peculiar to itself, as the shores of the Chesapeake. Of these, the most remarkable is the terrapin: it is about the size of a common land-tortoise, and haunts the shallow waters of the Bay, and the salt marshes around. They say, "he was a bold man who first ate an oyster;" a much more undaunted experimentalist was the first taster of the terrapin. I strongly advise no one to look at the live animal, till he has thoroughly learnt to like the savoury meat ; *then*, he will be enabled to laugh all qualms and scruples to scorn. Comparisons have been drawn between the terrapin and the turtle—very absurdly ; for, beyond the fact of both being testudines, there is not a point of resem-blance. Individually, I prefer the tiny ' diamond-back' to his gigantic congener, as more delicate and less cloying to the palate. Then there is the superb canvas-back, — peerless among water-fowl — never eaten in perfection out of sight of the sand-banks where he plucks the wild sea-celery ; and, in their due season, soft-crabs, and bay-mackerel. Last of all, there are oysters (woe worth the name !) of every shape, colour, and size. They assert that the cherry-stones are superior to our own Colchester natives in flavour : for reasons before stated, I cared not to contest the point.

A dinner based upon these materials, with a saddle of five-year-old mutton from the Eastern Shore as the main *pièce de résistance*, might have satisfied the defunct Earl Dudley, of fastidious memory. The wines deserve a separate paragraph.

For generations past, there has prevailed a great rivalry and emulation amongst the Amphitryons of Baltimore. They seem to have taken as much pride in their cellars as a Briton might do in his racing or hunting stables ; bestowing the same elaborate care on their construction and management. The prices given for rare brands appear fabulous, even to those who have heard, at home, three or four ' commissioners,' with plenipotentiary powers, disputing the favourite bin of some deceased Dean or Don. But, when you consider what the lost interest on capital lying dormant for seventy years will amount to, the apparent extravagance of cost is easily accounted for.

That is no uncommon age for Madeira. No European palate can form an idea of this wonderful wine; for, when in mature perfection, it is utterly ruined by transport beyond the seas. The vintages of Portugal and Hungary are thin and tame beside the puissant liquor that, after half a century's subjection to southern suns, enters slowly on its prime, with abated fire, but undiminished strength. Drink it then—and you will own, that from the juice of no other grape can be drawn such subtlety of flavour, such delicacy of fragrance passing the perfume of flowers. Climate of course is the first consideration. I believe Baltimore and Savannah limit, northward and southward, the region wherein the maturing process can be thoroughly perfected.

Madeira is their *spécialité*; but the wine-fanciers here can produce rare specimens of almost every vintage with the exception of Burgundy, which will not endure the long, rough voyage. There is a certain 'blue-seal' Johannisberg of 1844, far transcending any 'Schloss' wine that I have tasted; but the stock is nearly exhausted, and it is quite priceless.

Those pleasant banquets began early, about 5 p.m., and were indefinitely prolonged; for cigars are not supposed to interfere with the proper appreciation of Madeira, and the revellers here, cherish the honest old English custom, of chanting over their liquor. Closing my eyes now, so as to shut out the dingy drab walls of this my prison-chamber, I can call up one of those cheery scenes quite distinctly: I can hear the 'Chief's' voice close at my ear, trolling forth the traditional West Point ditty of "Benny Havens," or the rude sea-ballad, full of quaint pathos—

'Twas a Friday morning when we set sail:

then, deeper and fuller tones roll out Barry Corn-wall's sonorous verses of 'King Death.' It is good to look back on hours like these; though I doubt if the ill-cooked meats, whereof I hope soon to par-take—not unthankfully—will be improved by the memory.

In spite of this large hospitality, instances even of individual excess are comparatively rare. I have seen more aberration of intellect and convivial eccen-tricity after a Greenwich dinner, or a heavy 'guest-night,' than was displayed at any one of these Baltimore entertainments: a stranger endowed with a fair constitution, abstaining from morning drinks,

E

and paying attention to the Irishman's paternal
advice—' Keep your back from the fire, and don't
mix your liquors '—may take his place, with comfort
and confidence.

But my social recollections of Baltimore are by
no means exclusively bacchanalian. British Stock,—
lamentably at a discount in other parts of the Union,—
is, perhaps, a trifle above par here. The popularity
of our representatives—masculine and feminine—may
have something to do with this; at any rate, the
avenues of the best and pleasantest circles are easily
opened to any Englishman, of warranted position and
name.

If a traveller were to enter a drawing-room here,
expecting to be surprised at every turn by some
incongruity of speech or demeanour, such as book-
makers have attributed to our American Cousins,
he would not fill a page of his mental note-book. I
had no such prejudices to be disappointed : after
experience of society in many lands, I begin to think,
that well-bred and educated people speak and behave
after much the same fashion, all the world over.
Few Baltimorean voices are free from a perceptible
accent; it is more marked in the gentler sex, but
rarely so strong as to be disagreeable. The ear is
never offended by the New England twang or Connecticut drawl; while some tones rang true as silver.

You hear, of course, occasional peculiarities of expression, and words somewhat distorted from our

Anglican meaning, but these are not much more frequent or strange than provincial idioms at home. I was only once fairly puzzled—in this wise.

It was at a public 'assembly.' I had just been presented to the

Queen rose of a rosebud garden of girls,

a very Giselle, too, for litheness and grace; the music of the *Sirène* had begun, and my arm had circled my partner's willowy waist; when I felt her hang back, and saw on her fair face a distressed look of penitence and perplexity: "I'm so sorry," she murmured, "but I can't dance *loose*." Perfectly vague as to her meaning, I assured her that she should be guided after as *serrée* a fashion as she chose; but this evidently did not touch the difficulty. By the merest chance, I observed, that all the cavaliers put themselves, as it were, in position,—their left hand locked in the right of their *valseuse*,—before making a start, omitting the preliminary paces that get you well into the swing. It was all plain sailing then, and swift sailing too; the rest of the performance being completed with perfect unanimity, much to my own satisfaction, and, I trust, not to the discontent of my fairy-footed charge.

The freedom, and independent self-reliance of the Baltimorean demoiselles is very remarkable. At home, they receive and entertain their own friends, of either sex, quite naturally; and—taking their walks abroad,

or returning from an evening party—trust themselves
unhesitatingly to the escort of a single cavalier. Yet,
you would scarcely find a solitary imitation of the
'fast girls,' who have been giving our own ethical
writers so much uneasiness of late. It speaks well for
the tone of society, where such a state of things can
prevail, without fear and without reproach.   Though
Baltimore breeds gossips, numerous and garrulous as
is the wont of provincial cities, I never heard a
slander or a suspicion levelled against the most
intrepid of those innocent Unas.

From the *morale* one must needs pass to the *per-
sonnel*.   On the appearance of a *debutante*, they say,
the first question in Boston is, " Is she clever ? "   In
New York, " Is she wealthy ? "   In Philadelphia, " Is
she well-born ? "   In Baltimore, " Is she beautiful ? "
For many years past, common report has conceded
the Golden Apple to the Monumental City ; and I
think the distinction has been fairly won.

The small delicate features,—the long, liquid,
iridescent eyes,—the sweet, indolent *morbidezza*, that
make Southern beauty so perilously fascinating,—are
not uncommon here, and are often united to a clear-
ness and brilliancy of complexion scarcely to be found
nearer the tropics.   The Upper Ten Thousand by no
means monopolise these personal advantages.   At the
hour of ' dress parade ' you cannot walk five steps,
without encountering a face well worthy of a second
look.   Occasionally, too, you catch a provokingly

brief glimpse of a high slender instep, and an ankle
modelled to match it.   The fashion of Balmorals and
kilted kirtles prevails not here; both maids and matrons
are absurdly reluctant to submit their pedal perfec-
tions to the passing critic : even on a day when it is
a question of Mud *v.* Modesty, you may escort an
intimate acquaintance for an hour, and depart, doubt-
ing as to the colour of her hosen.   But—conceding
the justice of Baltimore's claim, and the constant
recurrence of more than a *stata pulchritudo*—I am
free to confess that, with a single exception, I saw
nothing approaching *supreme* perfection of form or
feature.

The exception was a very remarkable one.

I write these words, as reverently as if I were
drawing the portrait of the fair Austrian Empress, or
any other crowned beauty : indeed, I always looked
on that face, simply as a wonderful picture, and so I
remember it now.   I have never seen a countenance
more faultlessly lovely.   The *pose* of the small head, and
the sweep of the neck, resembled the miniatures of
Giulia Grisi in her youth, but the lines were more
delicately drawn, and the *contour* more refined ; the
broad open forehead, the brows firmly arched, without
an approach to heaviness, the thin chiselled nostril
and perfect mouth, cast in the softest feminine mould,
reminded you of the First Napoleon.   Quick mobility
of expression would have been inharmonious there :
yet with all its purity of outline, the face was not

severe or coldly statuesque,—only superbly serene, not lightly to be ruffled by any sudden revulsion of feeling ; a face, of which you never realised the perfect glory, till a pink-coral tint flushed faintly through clear pale cheeks ; while the lift of long trailing lashes revealed the magnificent eyes, lightening slowly up, to the full of their stormy splendour. It chanced, that the lady was a vehement Unionist, and ' rose,' very freely, on the subject of the war ; sincere in her honest patriotism, I doubt if she ever guessed at the real object of her opponent, in the arguments which not unfrequently arose.

If there be any indiscretion in this pen-and-ink sketch from nature, I should bitterly regret the involuntary error, though its subject, to the world in general, remains nameless as Lenore.

There is another peculiarity of Baltimore society, which a stranger will only perceive when he has passed withinside its porches. It is divided, not only into sets, but, as it were, into clans. Several of the leading families, generally belonging to the territorial aristocracy that took root in the State at, or soon after, its settlement, have so intermarried, as to create the most curious net of cousinship, the meshes of which are yearly becoming more intricate and numerous. Yet there are no especial indications of exclusiveness or spirit of *clique ;* rather it is the homely feeling of kinsmanship, which makes the intercourse of relations

more familiar and unceremonious, than that of intimate acquaintances or friends.

Cadets from many powerful houses in all the three
kingdoms, were among the early colonists of Maryland. It is good to mark, how gallantly the ' old
blood' holds its own, even here ; how, the descend-
ants of soldiers and statesmen have already attained
the pride of place, that their ancestors won at home
centuries ago, by a like valiance of sword, tongue,
or pen. Take one family, for instance, with whose
members I was fortunate enough to be especially
intimate.

For generations past, the Howards have been men
of mark in Maryland. Wherever hard or famous
work was to be done, in field or senate, one, at least,
of the name was sure to be found in the front. The
present head of the family sustains, right well, the
reputations of the worthies who went before him.
A staunch friend and an uncompromising adversary—
valuing political honesty no more lightly than private
honour—liberal and unsuspicious to a fault in his
social relations—very frank and simple in speech—
in manner always courteous and cordial—it would be
hard to find, in Europe, an apter representative of
the Ancien Régime. I believe, that those who
really know General Howard, will not consider this
sketch a flattery or an exaggeration. He was a
candidate for the Governorship at the last election,
and so powerful was his acknowledged personal

prestige, that, in despite of overt intimidation and
secret influences, which made a free-voting an absurdity, the Black Republicans exulted over his with-
drawal as an important victory.

Though ordinary business is so slack in Baltimore
just at present, almost every male resident, not engaged in law or physic, has, or supposes himself to
have, something to do. Instances of absolute idle-
ness are very rare. So, by ten A.M., all the men
betake themselves to their offices, and there busy
themselves about their affairs, after a fashion energetic or desultory, till after two o'clock. The dinner-
hour varies from three to half-past five. Post-prandial
labour is generally declined ; wisely, too, for few
American digestions will bear trifling with ; though
Nature must have gifted some of my acquaintance
with a marvellous internal mechanism. How, otherwise, could they stand a long unbroken course of
free living, with such infinitesimal correctives of
exercise ? The evening is spent after each man's
fancy,—at the club, or at one of the many houses
where a familiar is certain to meet a welcome, and
more or less of pleasant company. The entertainments are often more extensive and formal, embracing,
of course, music, and such are invariably wound up
by a supper. I have heard certain of our seniors grow
quite pathetic over the abolition of those social, if
unsalubrious, repasts. I wonder at such regrets no
longer, if I cannot share them. There is surely an

hilarious informality about these *media-nochi* that attaches to no antecedent feast; the freedom of a pic-nic, without its manifold inconveniences: as the witching hour draws nearer, the 'brightest eyes that ever have shone' glitter with a more liberal mirth ; and ' the sweetest lips that ever were kissed' sip the creaming Verzenay, or savour the delicate ' olio,' with a keener honesty of zest. The supper-tables are almost always adorned by some of the pretty, quaint conceits of an artist, whose fame extends far beyond Baltimore. Mr. Hermann's ice-imitations of all fruits and flowers, are marvellously vivid and natural : I have never seen them equalled by any continental *glaciers.*

I have lingered, perhaps, too long over too trifling details; and yet, I wish I had done my subject more justice. Be it remembered, that I visited Baltimore at a season of unusual social depression. I do not speak of the stagnation in commerce, and the ruin of Southern interests and possessions, from which many have suffered heavy pecuniary loss: the effects of the war come home to the Fair City yet more sharply. The prime of manhood is almost as rare now in her saloons, as it was in the Forum, when

> Sempronius Atratinus
>   Was left in charge at home
> With boys and with grey-headed men,
>   To keep the walls of Rome.

For months past, the best part of her *jeunesse dorée*

have been fighting,—as only the daintily born and
bred *can* fight, at bitter need,—in the van of Southern
armies.

Every fresh rumour of battle adds to the crowd of
pale anxious faces, and every bulletin lengthens the
list of mourners. There are few families, Federal or
Secessionist, who have not relatives—none that have
not dear friends—exposed to hourly peril, from disease, if not from lead or steel. The suspense felt in
England during the Crimean or Indian wars, cannot
be compared to that which many here are forced to
endure. *We* knew, at least, where our soldiers were,
and heard often how they fared: their sickness,
wounds, and deaths were all recorded. But the scenes
of this war's vast theatre are so often shifted, and communication with the remoter parts of the South-West
is so uncertain, that months will elapse without a line
of tidings from the absent; the grass has grown and
withered again, over many graves, before the weary
hearts at home knew that the time was past, for
waiting, and watching, and prayers.

The last season in New York, they say, has been
the gayest known for many years. The *nouveaux
riches* have been spending their ill or well gotten
gains, right royally. But the temptations to exuberant festivity, are few indeed in Baltimore, just now :
with all that they have to endure and fear, it speaks
well for the hardihood of her citizens, that they can
maintain even a chastened cheerfulness.

CHAPTER IV.

FRIENDS IN COUNCIL.

I MAY not deny that I found the places in which
my lines were just then cast exceeding pleasant : if
no serious purpose had been before me, I could have
been contented to sojourn there, till spring had waned.
But it is some satisfaction now, to be able to think
and say—I do say it, in perfect honesty and sincerity
—that I did not lose sight of my journey's main
object for one single day, from first to last.   Indeed, I
should have felt far more impatient of delay, had it
not been for the continuance of foul weather and
recurrence of heavy storms, which made armies, no
less than individuals, impotent to act or move.   On
the morning following my arrival I took counsel with
One who was, perhaps, better able to advise me as
to my future course than any other resident in
Baltimore : certainly none could have been more
heartily willing to help, both in word and deed.   I
owe to that man much more than a debt of ordinary
hospitality.   To say that his courtesy and cordi-
ality were marked, where benevolence to a stranger is
the rule—would very faintly express the personal

trouble he undertook and the personal risk he incurred, in his efforts to facilitate and further my purposes.   Up to this moment, I do not believe that he has grudged one whit of all this, much as he may have chafed at all having proved unavailing.   I am right sorry that prudence forbids my chronicling here a name which will always stand high on my muster-roll of friends ; but the memory of almost any Englishman who has visited Baltimore, will fill up the blank that I must leave, perforce.

It seemed that there was a choice of two routes into Secessia. The first—in many respects the easiest and far the most travelled—lay through the lower counties of Maryland : the narrow peninsula on which Leonards-town is situated forming the starting point, whence the blockade-runner attempted to cross the Lower Potomac—there, from four to eight miles wide.   It was necessary to run the gauntlet of several gun-boats and smaller craft;   but traffic at that particular time was carried on with tolerable regularity, and captures, though not unfrequent, were, so far, exceptions to a rule.   On the land route, before reaching the point of embarkation, lay the chief difficulties.   A horseman travelling with saddle-bags, became at once a suspicious personage, liable everywhere to jealous scrutiny.   The main roads were already becoming so cut up as to be traversed only with great toil and difficulty by ordinary vehicles, while the cross roads were simply impassable by

wheels. The principal turnpikes still hard enough to
carry a ' stage,' such as that from Washington to
Leonards-town, were more carefully guarded, and
picketed at certain points, especially bridges. At
any one of these points, a search might be appre-
hended, and anything beyond the simplest necessaries
was liable to seizure as contraband of war ; personal
arrest might possibly follow, but the Federal outposts were said to content themselves, as a rule, with
confiscation and appropriation, unless any documents
of a compromising nature were found : such a course
was obviously pleasanter for all parties, than sending
in prisoners—with their effects. Now it so chanced,
that in the modest—not to say scanty—outfit, which
I thought it worth while to bring out from home,
was a certain pair of riding-boots, by which I set
especial store. They were such as many of our field-
officers now in Canada are in the habit of wearing
—coming high up on the thigh, perfectly waterproof,
but very light, and pliant as a glove. I saw nothing
of American manufacture to compare with them.
Some of my duck-shooting acquaintance at Baltimore
were never weary of admiring their fair proportions ;
nor did my sage counsellor, before alluded to, refuse
his warm approbation ; but he urged very strongly
the hazard of my wearing them on my way to the
Lower Potomac : to carry or transmit them otherwise
was simply impossible. Nevertheless, neither Bom-
bastes nor Dalgetty could have clung more obstinately

to his favourite *chaussure* than did I to mine. I
knew that in the South, where an ordinary pair of
cavalry boots commands readily seventy dollars or
more, they could not be matched, and I had not

Lived in the saddle for years a score,

without learning that, on a long march, the value of
thoroughly well fitting and comfortable nether inte-
guments is 'above rubies.' And they did carry me
right well and safely through many rough ways and
much wild weather—impervious alike to water, mud,
rain or snow. Honour, where honour is due:
Fagg, of Panton Street, was the architect.* So I
'set my foot down,' literally and metaphorically, on
this point; absolutely determined that boots and
saddle-bags should share my fortunes. Eventually
I compromised things, by investing in a colossal
pair of overalls, warranted to smother and obli-
terate the proportions of any human legs, however
encased beneath.

But, during this discussion, the other route came
naturally into question. It was the one most generally
attempted by horsemen, and during the last ten weeks,
had been traversed repeatedly with perfect success.
It led through Howard and Montgomery counties to
the banks of the Upper Potomac, between Sugar-loaf

---

* If this looks like an advertisement, I can't help it, and can only
say that it is a disinterested one: it may be long before I need
water-proofs again, and I owe their deserving manufacturer
nothing but—justice.

Mountain and Seneca Creek. In this neighbourhood there were one or two fords, easily crossed at ordinary seasons, and only impassable after continuous downfalls of snow or rain. In fact, the chief obstacle was not the river, but the Chesapeake and Ohio canal, which runs close along the northern bank from Cumberland to Washington. This is not broad, but very deep, muddy, and precipitous, nor could I hear of any one who had succeeded in swimming a horse across it, or who had even made the attempt. The only passages were by bridges over, and culverts under, the water-way. These were of course jealously guarded; but it was possible, occasionally, to attack a picket with an irresistible ' silver spear;' and several instances had lately occurred of sentinels keeping their eyes and ears shut fast, during the brief time required for a small mounted party to pass their posts. I would not insinuate that venality was the general rule; so far from this being the case, I understood that it was necessary to make such overtures with great caution; the negotiation involving certain delay and possible failure. Detachments were constantly shifted from point to point, and regiments from station to station. Some corps were notoriously more accessible than others. According to common report, the recruits from New England, Massachusetts, and Connecticut were the easiest to deal with, and the subalterns were said to be usually open to a fair offer. But perhaps this was

a scandal after all; for the Marylander holds the
Yankee proper in such bitter dislike and contempt,
that he would miss no chance of a by-blow.

Once over the river at this point—you were comparatively safe. There were no regular pickets or patrols
on the further bank; only scattered reconnoitering parties of cavalry were to be evaded. Under cover of darkness, with a good local guide, this was easily done; and
one long night's ride brought you fairly into Secessia.

To this route my Mentor and I did at last seriously
incline, for good and sufficient reasons.

The Southern trooper's horse fares, I believe, far better in many ways than his Northern compeer. Besides
being more carefully groomed and tended, he carries a
rider better able to husband a failing animal's strength,
so as to 'nurse him home.' But the raiders travel
often far and fast through a country fetlock-deep on
light land, where provender is scanty and shelter
there is none. The daily wear and tear of horse-
flesh during this last bitter winter has been something fearful; even at the time I speak of the
difficulty of obtaining a really serviceable 'mount' in
Virginia could hardly be over-estimated. From 1000
to 1500 dollars were spoken of as ordinary prices for
a fair charger, and men willing to give that sum,
had been forced to go into South Carolina before
they could suit themselves. In my own case the
difficulty was increased; for—in hard condition,
without cloak, valise, or accoutrements—I draw

14 st. 10 lb., in a common hunting-saddle. Now, an animal well up to that weight, with anything like action or a turn of speed, is right hard to find on the Transatlantic seaboard. Even in Maryland, where horse-flesh is comparatively plenty, and breeders of blood-stock abound, such a specimen is a rarity: among the stallions, I can scarcely remember one coming up to the standard of a real weight-carrier, with the exception of Black Hawk. I saw hundreds of active, wiry hackneys, excellently adapted for fast, *light* work, either in shafts or under saddle; their courage and endurance, too, are beyond question; but—looking at them with a view to long, repeated marches, where, if ever, you ought to have a few pounds in hand—I decided that they were about able to carry, the boots honourably mentioned above. After mature consideration and long debate, it was settled that I should, if possible, be mounted before starting, instead of trusting to chance beyond the Border. This, of course, decided the selection of routes: no quadruped could cross the Lower Potomac.

Some scores of miles up the country, there lived, and, I trust, lives still, a certain small horse-dealer, a firm Secessionist at heart, well versed in the time-tables of the road southward; indeed, his house was, as it were, a principal station on the Underground Railway. He was reputed trustworthy, and fairly honest in traffic. I can endorse this, conscientiously,

F

only hoping that such a remarkable characteristic as
the last-named will not identify the individual to his
hurt.   I was at once put into communication with Mr.
—— Symonds—let us call him, for the sake of old
hippic memories.   He spoke confidently as to my
ultimate prospects of getting across, without pretend-
ing to fix an exact day, or even week.   Shortly
before my arrival he had forwarded several travellers,
who arrived at their journey's end without let or
hindrance : I suppose there is no indiscretion in
saying, that Lord Hartington and Colonel Leslie were
among the fortunate ones.   Mr. Symonds " thought
he had something that would suit me ; " so a few
days later, the animal and the dealer paraded for
inspection in Baltimore.

I was much pleased with both.   The man seemed
to understand his business thoroughly ; without
making extravagant promises, he expressed himself
willing to serve my purpose to the utmost of his
power, at any reasonable risk to himself ; and spoke
very moderately about the horse, asking for nothing
more than a fair trial of his merits.   I liked the
animal better than anything I had seen, so far.   He
was a dark-brown gelding, about 15·3, with strong
square hind-quarters, and a fair slope of shoulder ;
without much knee-action ; but springy enough in
his slow paces ; his turn of speed was not remarkable,
but he could last for ever, and, if the ground were not
too heavy, would gallop on easily for miles with a

long, steady stride; like most Maryland-bred horses, he had wonderfully clean, flat legs ; after the hardest day's work I never saw a puff on them; he was not sulky or savage, but had a temper and will of his own; both of these, however, yielded, after a sharp wrangle or two, to the combined influence of coaxing and a pair of sharp English rowels; in the latter days of our acquaintance we never had a difference of opinion. Considering the scarcity of stanch horse-flesh, the price asked was very moderate, and I closed the bargain on the spot. I was assured that my new purchase was of the Black Hawk stock, and he was christened ' Falcon ' that same day.

So Symonds departed, promising to set all possible wheels to work, and to inform me of the earliest opportunity for a start ; the first *desideratum* being, of course, a reliable guide.

I cannot say that the hours of my detention hung heavily. The social attractions of the place were ample enough to fill up afternoons and evenings right pleasantly : in the mornings, whenever the weather was not pitilessly bad, I rode or drove through the country round.

I think no one understands the full luxury of rapid motion without bodily exertion, till they have sate behind a pair of first-class American trotters. The waggon, to begin with, is a mechanical triumph : it is wonderful, to see such lightness combined with such strength and stability. I saw one, after

five years' constant usage over fearfully bad roads : it
was owned by a man noted for reckless pace, where
many Jehus drove furiously ; not a bolt or joint had
started ; the hickory of shafts and spokes still seemed
tough as hammered steel. These carriages are roomy
enough, and fairly comfortable, when you are in them;
but that same entrance is apt rather to puzzle a
stranger. The fore and hind wheels are nearly the
same height, and set very close together; even when
the fore-carriage is turned so that they nearly lock,
the space left for ascent between them is narrow
indeed ; this same arrangement renders, of course,
impossible, a sudden turn in a contracted circle. But
the dames and demoiselles who put their trust in
these chariots, make a mock at such small difficulties.
You are shamed into activity, after once seeing your
fair charge spring to her place, with graceful confidence, never soiling the skirt of her dainty robe.

    The team that I used to drive constantly, were
fair, but not remarkable performers ; their best
mile-time was a trifle under 3·20. Their owner had
not had leisure to keep them in steady exercise,
so at first they were very skittish, and prone to
break ; but they soon settled down to their work,
and then did not pull an ounce too much for pleasure,
even when spinning along at top-speed, with their small
lean heads thrust eagerly forward, after the fashion of
the barbs called ' Drinkers of the Wind.' Once I
drove, in single harness, a trotter whose time was close

on 2·45 ; but this is not considered anything extraordinary, and the outside price of such an animal
would be about 1000 dollars : once—'inside the
forties '—the fancy prices begin, and go up rapidly
to 4000 dollars, or higher.

It must be remembered that the roads in these
parts cannot be compared, either for level or metal,
with the highways over our own champaign; they
' cut up ' fast in rough weather, and settle slowly ;
while the ground generally sinks and swells too abruptly
to allow of a lengthened stretch at full speed. I
often wished that the whole turn-out of which I
have spoken could be transported, without the risk of
sea-passage, into one of our Eastern counties. I can
hardly conceive a greater luxury to a ' coachman,'
than sending such a pair along, on the road leading
into Norfolk from Newmarket.

I had been some time in Baltimore before I was
honoured by an introduction to the most renowned—
it is a bold word—of all its beauties. To many,
even in England, the name of Flora Temple will
not sound strange : her great feat of the mile in two
minutes nineteen seconds has never yet been equalled,
and for the last three years she has rested idly on
her laurels, in default of any challenger to dispute her
sovereignty of the turf. Her owner, W. Macdonald,
Esq., resides within a short distance of the city, and,
I doubt not, would receive any stranger with the
same courtesy that he extended to me. His stables

are well worth a visit, for, besides the fair champion, they contain several other trotters of no mean repute, (one team, the " Chicago Chestnuts," is a notoriety); and the carriages exemplify every improvement of American manufacture. The building itself is very peculiar—perfectly circular, with a diameter of 100 feet, and a dome-roof rising to fifty feet at the crown. In the centre is a large fountain of white marble, round which is a broad tan-ride ; outside this again are the stalls, horse-boxes, harness, and carriage apartments.

On the left-hand side of the entrance-arch is a large chamber, rush-strewn, like the tiring-room of some ancient châtelaine, but brilliant with polished wood and metal, gorgeous with stained glass : that is the boudoir of the Queen of the Turf, and over the doorway are her titles of honour emblazoned. The Great Lady—as is the wont of her compeers—is somewhat capricious at times, and disinclined to parade her beauty before strangers ; but she chanced to be in a special good humour that day, and allowed me to admire her points at leisure.

It is hard to fancy a more faultless picture of compact activity and strength. Viewed from a distance, and at first sight, her proportions deceive everyone ; you are surprised, indeed, when you come close to her withers, and find that you are standing by a veritable pony, barely touching 14·3. But look at the long slope of shoulder — the chest, wide enough to give the largest lungs free play in their labour—the flat, square quarters, the muscular fulness of the upper-limbs, so perfectly 'let down '— the clear sinewy legs, without a curb-mark or wind-fall to tell tales of fearfully fast work and hard training —and you will wonder less how the Championship was won. They say that the Queen was never fitter than now; yet, since her hot youth she has seldom rested, and now, long past the equine climacteric, is far advanced in her teens.

This part of America is so constantly visited by my compatriots, that it may be well, while we are on this subject, to say a few words about the sporting resources of Maryland.

There is very fair partridge-shooting in many districts. As I crossed the country in mid-winter, I could hardly judge of what the autumn cover would be; but I heard that of this there was no lack; in October the birds will lie right well, especially in the weedy stubbles, and along the brushy banks of water-courses. In many places a fair shot may reckon on from ten to fifteen brace, and I could name two guns that have not unfrequently bagged from thirty to fifty brace on the Eastern shore; but, I believe, they shot with unusually straight powder. There is a good show of wood-cock at certain seasons; but it sounds strange to English ears when they speak of the season opening in June : the bird is much smaller than ours, averaging about seven or eight ounces, and it is found much oftener in comparatively open ground than in thick woodland.

The royal sport of Maryland is, the wild-fowl shooting on the Chesapeake Bay. The best of the season was passed long before my arrival; but in two visits to Carroll's Island I saw enough to feel sure that my Baltimore friends vaunted not its capabilities in vain. I cannot remember having seen elsewhere so promising a ' ducking-point.' Imagine a low, marshy peninsula; verging landward into stunted woods, full of irregular water-courses and stagnant pools; tapering off seaward into a mere spit of sand, on which reeds and bent-grass scarcely deign to grow: towards the extreme point, just where the neck is narrowest, are the ' blinds,'—ten or twelve in number—a long gun-shot apart, in which the fowlers lurk, waiting for their prey. On either side stretch the broad estuary of the Gunpowder River, and the broader waters of the Chesapeake, along whose shallows lie the banks of wild celery on which the canvass-back loves to feed. Changing these feeding-grounds soon after dawn and shortly before sunset, the fowls naturally cross the neck of the little peninsula: they will never willingly pass over land, unless they can see water close beyond. Occasionally you may have fair shooting all through the day; but, as a rule, the above-mentioned hours are those alone when good ' flying ' may be reckoned on. When it *is* good, the sport must be superb: it is the very sublimation of ' rocketing.' You must hold straight and forward, to stop a cock-pheasant whirring over the leafless tree-tops,—well up in the keen January wind ; but a swifter traveller yet is the canvass-back drake, as he swings over the bar, at the fullest speed of his whistling pinions, disdaining to turn a foot from his appointed course, albeit vaguely suspecting the ambush below. The height of the ' flying ' varies, of course, greatly. I saw nothing brought down, to the best of my calculation, within forty-five or fifty yards, and most were much beyond that distance. At first, you let several chances slip, believing them to be out of shot ; but the mighty duck-guns, carrying five or six drams of strong coarse powder, do their work gallantly ; and nothing can be more refreshing than the *aplomb*, with which their victims, stricken down from that dizzy height, strike water, reeds, or sand.

Among the many varieties of fowl—varying from wild swan to widgeon—that are slain here, the canvass-back holds, by common consent, the pre-eminence for delicacy of flavour and tenderness of meat; but I confess I have thought almost as highly of an occasional ' red-head' in perfect condition.

This, the most celebrated of all ducking points on the Chesapeake, is rented by a club, the members of which are all resident in Baltimore, or its neighbour-hood : the number, I think, is limited to twelve. When they muster in force, the sleeping accommodation must necessarily be limited, as Mr. Russell describes it; but there is room and verge enough in the quaint old homestead, for any ordinary party. The burly host himself is quite in keeping with the place, and bears his part right jovially in the rough-and-ready revels, that contrast not disagreeably, with the social amenities left behind in the city. I spent some very pleasant hours of sunshine and twilight at the 'Colonel's;' (he has as good a right to the title as many more pretentious dignitaries); though the flying was indifferent on both my visits. On the first occasion, though several varieties of fowl were bagged, we only secured one canvass-back, which was courteous enough to tumble to the stranger's gun. Sooth to say, the first inter-view with the uncompromising contraband who wakes you *is* a trial, and it is bitterly cold work for feet and fingers, when you first come into your 'blind' under the early dawn; but the blood soon warms up as the warning cries from the markers become more frequent; the pulse quickens as the dark specks or lines loom nearer, defined against the dull red or silvery grey of the sky-line; chills and shivers are all forgotten, as your first 'red-head'—pioneer of a whole 'skein' from the river—crashes down yards behind you, on the hard, wet sand that fringes the bay.

In the genial October weather, during which comes the cream of the flying, the sojourn at Carroll's

Island must be really delightful. But, much I
fear, that next autumn's prospects look brighter for
the fowl, than for their sedulous persecutors. Who
can say, what changes may not have been wrought in
the fortunes of some of those cheery sportsmen, before
next season shall open? Perhaps, ere that, the echoes
of the Chesapeake will be waked by an artillery that
would drown the roar even of the mighty duck-guns.
The sea-fishing in the bay is remarkably good, but it
is not greatly affected by amateurs; and very few
yachts are seen on its usually placid waters. Almost
all the streams round the Chesapeake, in spite of
their being perpetually 'thrashed,' and never preserved, abound in small trout; but farther a-field, in
North-western Maryland, where the tributaries of
the Potomac and Shenandoah flow down the woody
ravines of Cheat Mountain and the Blue Ridge, there
is room for any number of fly-rods, and fish heavy
enough to bend the stiffest of them all.

Before troubles began, they used to hunt, after a
fashion, in most of the upland districts; but the sport
can hardly be very exciting. The gravest of the
'potterings' of ancient days, when our great-grand-
sires used to drag up to their fox while the dew
lay heavy on the grass, was a 'cracker,' compared to
one of these runs, as I heard them described. Three
or four couple of cross-bred hounds do occasionally
weary and worry to death their unhappy quarry, after
three or four hours 'ringing' through endless wood-

lands; unless, indeed, he goes earlier to ground, in which case he is dug out to meet a quicker and more merciful death. The fact, that a heavy fall of snow is supposed greatly to facilitate matters, about settles the question of sport. I should like to ask Charles Payne, or Goddard, his opinion of ' pricking ' a fox. However, to ride straight and fast over such a country would be simply impossible: the detestable snake-fences meet you everywhere, with their projecting ' zigzags ' of loosely-piled rails; you can hardly ever get a chance of taking them in your stride, and they are a fair standing-jump with the top bar removed, which generally involves dismounting. The name of poor Falcon has led me so far a-field, that I must continue my own chronicle in another chapter.

CHAPTER V.

In about ten days I heard from Symonds. The road was not yet open, but a party was waiting to start. He had secured me a henchman, in the shape of a private in an Alabama regiment who was anxious to accompany any one South, without fee or reward. The man was said to be well acquainted with the country beyond the Potomac, besides being really honest and courageous. I had no reason to question these qualifications, though his tongue was apt to stir too loudly for prudence, and too fast for truth; while over the manner of his release (he had been for some months a prisoner of war), there hung a mystery never cleared up satisfactorily. It was necessary, of course, that my squire should be mounted, and after some deliberation, it was settled that I should furnish him with a steed. I was moved thereto, partly from a wish to spare Falcon all dead-weight in the shape of saddle-bags, partly from the knowledge that superfluous horseflesh was a commodity easily and profitably disposed of in Secessia. I did not trouble myself much about my second

horseman's mount, merely stipulating for a moderate
animal at a moderate price. I bought, indeed, in the
dark, and did not see my purchase till the day before
our first actual start. This last negotiation concluded
—I had nothing to do but to abide patiently till it
pleased others to sound ' boot and saddle.'

So day followed day till, in spite of all the social
attractions of Baltimore, I began to chafe bitterly
under the delay. I never could get rid of a half-guilty
consciousness that I ought to be somewhere else,
and that somewhere,—far away. On the morning
of 17th February, I was in the office of my friend and
chief-counsellor above mentioned, discussing the propriety of throwing aside the upper route altogether—
selling back my cattle — and making my way as
straight as possible to the shores of the Lower
Potomac. We were actually debating the point
when the door opened, and disclosed Symonds. He
had come down in hot haste, to tell us that a main
obstacle was removed. The water had been let out
of the Chesapeake and Ohio canal, so that it could
now be easily crossed at any unguarded point. The
picket was of necessity so widely scattered as to be
easily evaded. The small party that my squire and I
were to join meant starting, at latest on the following
Friday or Saturday night. Symonds had no recent intelligence from the immediate bank of the
river; but he believed that, in despite of the heavy
rains and occasional snow-storms, we should find one

crossing-place—White's Ford, to wit,—still barely practicable.

I was already furnished with saddlery, etc., but small final preparations and divers leave-takings filled up every spare minute, till afternoon on the following day. I was to sleep the first night at a house only a few miles from Symonds's, so as to be in readiness to start at two hours' notice, and my Mentor insisted on seeing me so far on my way. It had been snowing at intervals all the morning, and the flakes were driving thick and blindingly as we drove out of Baltimore : our team faced the heavy road and frequent hills gallantly ; but the fifteen miles seemed long, that brought us to the door of our quarters— faces aching with the lash of sleet,—beard and moustaches frozen to bitterness.

As my hosts were in nowise privy to my plans, I may venture to say, that for the next three days I was more or less a guest at Drohoregan Manor. This ancient homestead of the Carroll family is very well described by Mr. Russell in his "Diary:" his visit however, was to the late possessor, who died last year. The law of primogeniture does not prevail here, and it was only an accidental succession of single heirs, that brought an undivided patrimony down to the present generation. One cannot help regretting, that the estate is to be cut up, now, into five shares or more. Eleven thousand acres of fertile hill and dale, sinking and swelling gently, so as to attract all the

benignity of sun or breeze, not more densely wooded
than is common on our own Western shores, and
watered to an ornamental perfection; truly, on any
civilized land, such is a goodly heritage.

The home-farm of Drohoregan Manor has long
been celebrated for the breeding of a high-class stock
of all kinds. I saw sheep there scarcely coarser than
the average of South-downs; and some fine, level,
clean-limbed steers. Here has stood, for a dozen
years past, the renowned Black Hawk, considered
by many superior to his sire, the Morgan stallion
of the same name. He realised my idea of a
thorough-bred weight-carrier, better than anything
I saw in Maryland; though if one of his stock—a
brown two-year-old colt— 'furnishes' according to
present promise, he will probably be surpassed in his
turn. There were a large number of colts and fillies
well adapted for rapid road work; I was not
surprised to hear that at the sale which followed
quickly on my visit, they fetched more than average
prices. I did not think so highly of the cart stock,
principally the produce of a big grey Percheron horse.
Both he and Black Hawk remain in their present
quarters; for the late Colonel Carroll's eldest son
retains the Manor House, and proposes, I believe, to
continue both the farming and breeding establishments on no diminished scale. I rode up to Mr.
Symonds's in the afternoon of the 19th; he was
absent, but his wife informed me, that it was

possible, though scarcely probable, that our party would start the following night. Then, for the first time, I made acquaintance with my squire for the nonce—'Alick,' he was called; I cannot remember his surname: he had a rugged, honest face, and a manner to match; but I was rather disconcerted at hearing, that he knew no more of riding or stable-work than he had picked up in a fortnight's irregular practice, in an establishment where horses as well as men were taught to rough it in good earnest.

I liked my new purchase much worse than my new acquaintance. The former was a raw-boned, leggy roan, with a coarse head, a dull eye, and a weakish neck, far too low in condition, as I saw and said at once, for long travel through a country where a horse must needs lose flesh daily, from pure lack of provender. However, there was no time to make a change, so I was fain to hope that easy journeys at first, and a light weight on his back, might gradually bring the ungainly beast into better form. It appeared that he was just recovering from the distemper and 'sore tongue,' which had followed each other in rapid succession. These two diseases are the terror of Virginian and Maryland stables. An animal who has once surmounted them is supposed to be seasoned, and acquires considerable additional value, like a 'salted' horse in Southern Africa.

So I returned to the Manor for that night, and

thither, early the next morning, came Symonds in
person. He informed me, that the start from his
house would not take place till after nightfall on the
following evening; so that I had thirty vacant hours
before me.   I knew that the last English mail had
reached Baltimore, and it then seemed so uncertain
when letters would reach me again, that I could not
resist the temptation of securing my correspondence.
My host was himself returning to the city; so I
accepted the offer of a seat in his waggon, and we
had a pleasant drive back through the clear frosty
weather.

The next day, — having made the Post-office
' part,' and said those few more last words that
are forgotten at every leave-taking,—I retraced my
steps, by the afternoon train, to Ellicott's Mills, where
I found a carriage from Drohoregan Manor awaiting
me.   At this point, the Patapsco hurries through a
channel narrowed by embankments and encroach-
ments of the granite cliffs. Looking upon the yellow
water streaked with huge foam-clots, chafing against
its banks lip high—I could not but augur ill for
our chances of traversing a wider and wilder stream.
But it was too early then to think of desponding, so
casting forebodings behind, I drove up to our rally-
ing place, rattling over four long leagues under
seventy minutes : the black ponies tossed their
heads, and champed their bits gaily, as they made
best time over the last mile.

I found that the party that purposed actually to cross the Potomac, was, from one cause or another, reduced to four, including myself and my attendant. A cousin of Symonds's, hight Walter, with the same surname—there is a perfect clan of them in those parts—was to accompany us only to our first resting place, a farmhouse about eighteen miles off. Our proposed companions were both Maryland men; one had already served for some months in a regiment of Confederate cavalry, and was returning to his duty, after one of those furloughs—often self-granted—in which the Borderers are prone to indulge; the other was a mere youth, and had never seen a shot fired; but a more enthusiastic recruit could hardly be conceived.

Twilight had melted into darkness long before the rest of the party arrived; then an hour or more was consumed in the last preparations and refreshments. It was fully nine o'clock on the night of February 21st, when we started from Symonds's door—strengthened for the journey with a warm stirrup-cup, and warmer kind wishes from the family, including two *very* sympathising damsels, who had come in from neighbouring homesteads to bid the Southward-bound good speed.

When we had ridden a mile, the Marylanders turned off to a house where they were to take up some letters, promising to rejoin us before we had gone a league. But we traversed more than that

distance, at the slowest foot-pace, without being over-
taken, and at length determined to wait for the
laggards, drawing back about thirty paces off the
path, into a glade where there was partial shelter from
the icy wind that swept past, laden with coming
snow.   There we tarried for a long half-hour (told on
my watch by a fusee-light), and still no signs of our
companions.   Symonds, the cousin, who abode with
us still, began to mutter doubts, and the Alabama
man to grumble curses (he had ever a fatal facility in
blasphemy); I own to having entertained divers
disagreeable misgivings, though I carefully avoided
expressing them.   At last, our guide thought it best
that we should make our way to a lonely farmhouse,
about seven miles short of our night's destination,
where, in any case, the party was to have called in
passing.   So we wound on through the narrow wood-
paths in single file—sinking occasionally pastern-deep,
where the thin ice over mud-holes supplanted the safe
crackling snow-crust — traversing frequent fords,
where rills were swollen into brooks and turbid
streams.   Some of those gullies must have been dark
even at noon-day, with overhanging cypress and pine;
they were so bitterly black now that you were fain to
follow close on the splash in your front, for no mortal
ken could have pierced half a horse's length ahead.

   At length, we left the path altogether, and,
pulling down a snake-fence, passed through the gap
into open fields.   It was all plain sailing here, and a

great relief after groping through the dim woodland ; we encountered no obstacle but an occasional zigzag, easily demolished, till we came to a deep hollow, where the guide dismounted—evidently rather vague as to his bearings—and proceeded to feel his way. Somewhere about here there was a 'branch' (or rivulet) to be crossed, and danger of bog if you went astray. At last he professed to have discovered the right point; but neither force nor persuasion would induce the stubborn brute he rode to face it. There was nothing for it, but trying what 'giving him a lead' would do. The place was evidently a small one, but the landing absolutely uncertain; so I put Falcon at it steadily, letting him have his head. Then first my poor horse displayed his remarkable talent for getting over difficulties in the dark, a talent that I have never seen equalled in any other animal, and which alone made him invaluable. He took off—almost at a stand—out of clay up to his hocks, exactly at the right time, and landed me on firm ground without a scramble. A minute afterwards there came a rush, a splutter, and a crash, and a struggling mass rolled at my feet; gradually resolving itself into a man, a roan horse, and two saddlebags. So sped Alabama's maiden leap. It was soft falling, and no harm beyond the breaking of a strap was done; but it was fully three quarters of an hour before our united efforts got **Symonds's** refuse across. We accomplished it at last, by hurling the brute backwards into the branch with main strength, and then wading ourselves through mud that just touched the upper edge of my thigh-boots.   Once over, the track was easily found, and a barking chorus, performed by half-a-dozen vigilant mongrels, guided us up to the homestead we were seeking, just as the snow began to fall heavily.

The stout farmer was soon on foot—men sleep lightly in these troublous times—proffering food, fire, and shelter.   Our guide strongly advised our remaining there, till we could gain some tidings of our lost companions : it seemed so unlikely that they should have passed or missed us on the road, that he could not but fear lest accident or treachery should have detained them ; he offered himself to retrace our track, and make all inquiries, which he—alone—could do safely.   So it was settled ; and, after making the horses as comfortable as rude accommodation would allow, my squire and I betook ourselves to rest, not unwillingly, about 3 a.m.

Every traveller's first waking impulse leads him straight to the window or to the weather-glass.   I turned away from the look-out in utter disgust ; trees a hundred yards off were invisible through the cloud of driving snow-flakes ; and a level white mantle, rising up to the lower bars of the snake-fences, merged tillage into pasture undistinguishably.   I chronicled that same day, as the dreariest of all *then* remembered Sabbaths. Besides some odd numbers of an ancient Methodist

magazine, there was no literature available; all
the letters that I cared to write, had been despatched
before I left Baltimore.

A visit to the shed which sheltered our horses, did
not greatly raise one's spirits. Poor Falcon was hardy
as a Shetlander, and in any ordinary weather I never
thought of clothing him; but no wonder he shivered
there, under a rug, coated inch-deep with snow; the
rough-hewn sides and crazy roof gaping with fissures
a hand-breadth wide and more, were scanty defence
against the furious drift, which swept through, not to
be denied. I tried to comfort my horse, by chafing
his legs and ears till both were thoroughly warm,
setting Alick at the same task with the roan; though
clumsy and apt to be obstinate, he worked with a will.
At last we had the satisfaction of seeing both animals
feed, with an appetite that I, for one, could not but envy.
Our hosts were so cordial in their honest hospitality,
that one felt ungrateful in being so wearily bored.

In the afternoon we had a visit from a neighbouring farmer, who, I believe, had been summoned with the benevolent intent that he should
enlighten or entertain the stranger. He was one of
those stout, elderly men, who, by dint of a certain
portliness of presence, gravity of manner, and slowness
of speech, acquire in their own country much honour
for social or political wisdom. He was quite up to the
average rank of rustic oracles; nevertheless, our converse dragged heavily; it was 'up hill all the way.'

There was a depressing formality about the whole
arrangement; my interlocutor sat exactly opposite
to me, putting one cut-and-dried question after another; never removing his eyes from my face, while I
answered to the best of my power, save to glance at
the silent audience, as though praying them to note
such and such points carefully. I began to feel as
I did in the Schools long ago, when the *vivâ voce*
examiner was putting me through my facings; and
was really glad when the one-sided dialogue ended.
The queries were very simple for the most part, relating chiefly to the sympathies and intentions of Great
Britain with regard to the war. On the latter point
I could, of course, give no information beyond vague
surmises, practically worthless; as to the former, I
thought myself justified in saying that the balance
of public feeling, in the upper and agricultural classes
especially, leant decidedly Southward. But here, as
elsewhere, I found it impossible to make Secessionists
understand or allow the wisdom, justice, or generosity
of the non-interference policy hitherto pursued by our
government. This is not the time or place to discuss
an important question of statecraft, nor am I pre-
sumptuous enough to assert that different and more
decisive measures would have had all the good effect
that their advocates insist upon; but, however justi-
fiable England's conduct may have been according to
theories of international law, I fear the practical result
will be, that she has secured the permanent enmity of

one powerful people, and the discontented distrust of
another. It is ill trusting even proverbs implicitly;
that old one, about the safe Middle Course, will break
down, like the rest, sometimes. My pertinacious
querist stopped, I suppose, when he had got to the
end of his list, and apparently spent the rest of the
evening in a slow process of digestion; for he would
break out, now and then, at the most irrelevant times,
with a repetition of one of his former interrogations,
which I had to answer again, briefly as I might.

About sundown *le Bon Gualtier* returned, sorely
travel-worn himself, and with an utterly exhausted
horse. He had ascertained that our companions had
gone on, probably to our original destination of the
previous night; though, why they should have passed
our present resting-place without calling there, remained a mystery; nor was that point ever satisfactorily explained. To proceed at once was impossible,
for a fresh horse had to be found for our guide; this,
a cousin of our host's offered to provide by the following evening (we could not venture to stir abroad in
daylight); he also offered to make his way to the farm
where the missing men were supposed to be, early
in the morning, and to bring back certain intelligence
of their movements. This was only one instance of
the cordial kindness and hearty co-operation which I
met with at the hands of these sturdy yeomen. Not
only would they rise and open their doors at the
untimeliest of hours, and entertain you with their

choicest of fatlings, corn, and wine, but there was no
amount of personal toil or risk that they would not
gladly undergo to forward any southward-bound
stranger on his way; nor could you have insulted
your host more grossly, than by hinting at pecuniary
guerdon.   Before midnight the snow had ceased to
fall; the next morning broke bright and sunny,
though the frost still held on sharply.   Two or three
visitors, masculine and feminine, came in sleighs
during the day, and altogether it passed much more
rapidly than the preceding one.   About 4 p.m. the
good-natured messenger returned: our comrades
had duly reached the spot originally fixed for the
Saturday night's halt, and had pursued their journey
on the Sunday evening to the farm which was to be
our last point before attempting the Potomac; their
written explanation was very vague, but they promised
to wait for us at the house they were then making
for.   We at once determined to press on thus far that
night, though the score or more of miles of crow-flight
between would certainly be lengthened, at least a
third, by the *détours* necessary to avoid probable
pickets or outposts, and the deep snow must make
the going fearfully heavy.   Walter's fresh mount
came down—a powerful, active mare, in good working
condition; but with weak, cracked hoofs that would
not have carried her a day's march on hard, stony
roads.

Under the red sunset we started once more, with

more good wishes; indeed, I had ridden a mile, before my fingers forgot the parting hand-grip of my stalwart host.

Now in thinking or speaking of these night rides beforehand, one is apt to invest them with a slight tinge of romance and excitement, which is not unattractive. Let me say, that in practice nothing can be more drearily disagreeable. I can fancy a canter over the same woodland paths, under the capricious light of a broad summer or autumn moon, with one or more pleasant companions, being both exhilarating and agreeable; but traverse the same number of miles in a night of winter or early spring; when you have to blunder on at a foot's pace in Indian file, thankful, indeed, when the snow or mud is only fetlock deep; where, if you are in mood for conversation, you dare not often speak above a whisper (I never could see the sense of this, far out in the wilds, but the guides are imperative); where the solitary excitement is found in the possible proximity of a picket, or the probable depth of a ford. I think you would agree with me, that the only object in the journey on which your eyes or thoughts delight to dwell, is the 'biggit land' that ends it.

On that especial night, we had one thing in our favour; the reflection from the fresh white ground carpet would have prevented darkness, even without the light of a waxing moon. But it was slow and weary travelling. It would have been cruelty to have forced the horses beyond a walk through snow that in places was over their knees; besides which, we dared not risk a jingle of stirrup or bridle-bit, where an outlying picket might be within ear-shot. Twice we passed within twenty yards, of where the fresh track showed that the patrol had recently turned at the end of his beat; but the guide knew the country thoroughly, and professed to have no fears. To speak the truth, I had heard him, when in the ingle-nook, and warm with Old Rye, vaunt so loudly his own sagacity and courage, that I conceived certain misgivings as to how far either was to be relied on. That night, however, he fully maintained part of his character, by leading us safely and surely through a perfect labyrinth of tracks; sometimes diverging across the open country, and occasionally plunging into woodland where there was no vestige of a path.

I ought to be nearly weather-proof by this time; but, in spite of a warm riding-cloak and a casing of chamois leather from neck to ankle, I felt sometimes chilled to the marrow; my lips would hardly close round the pipe-stem; even while I smoked the breath froze on my moustache, stiff and hard. My flask was full of raw country whisky, fiery hot from the still; but it seemed at last to have lost all strength, and was nearly tasteless. I would have given anything for a brisk trot or rattling gallop to break the monotonous foot-pace; but the reasons

before stated forbade the idea: there was nothing
for it, but to plod steadily onwards. Walter himself
suffered a good deal in hands and feet; the
Alabama man, utterly unused to the lower extremes
of temperature, only found relief from his misery in
an occasional drowsiness that made him sway helplessly in his saddle. The last league of our route
lay through the White Grounds. The valley of the
Potomac widens here towards the north, and 6,000
acres of forest stretch away—unbroken, save by rare
islets of clearings. There was no visible track; but
our guide struck boldly across the woodland, taking
bearings by certain landmarks and the steady moon.
It was not dark even here; but low sweeping boughs
and fallen trunks often hidden by snow, made the
travelling difficult and dangerous. I ceased not to
adjure Alick, who followed close in my rear, to keep
fast hold of his horse's head. I doubt if he ever
heard me, for he never intermitted a muttered
running-fire of the most horrible execrations that I
ever listened to, even in this hard-swearing country.
Whether this ebullition of blasphemy comforted him
at the moment I cannot say; but, if 'curses come
home to roost,' a black brood was hatched that night,
unless one whole page be blotted out from the register
of the Recording Angel.

Both men and horses rejoiced, I am sure, when,
about 2 a.m., we broke out into a wide clearing, and
drew rein under the lee of outbuildings surrounding

the desired homestead. The farmer was soon aroused, and came out to give us a hearty though whispered welcome. It is not indiscreet to record *his* name, for he has already 'dree'd his doom;' he was noted among his fellows for cool determination in purpose and action; truly, I believe that the yeomanry of Maryland counts no honester or bolder heart, than stanch George Hoyle's.

Our lost companions were sleeping placidly upstairs; that was the best intelligence that our host could give us. He laughed at the idea of fording the Potomac, declaring that no living man or horse could stand, much less swim, in the stream. Knowing the character of the man, and his thorough acquaintance with the locality, one ought to have accepted his decision unquestioned; but I was not then so inured to disappointment as I became in later days, and wished to see for myself how the water lay. After a short sleep and hurried breakfast, Hoyle took me to a point whence we looked down on a long reach of the river. At the first glance through my field-glasses, every vestige of hope vanished. The fierce current —its sullen neutral tint chequered with frequent foam-clots—washed and weltered high against its banks, eddying and breaking savagely wherever it swept against jut of ground or ledge of rock; while ever and anon, shot up above the turbid surface a tossing trunk of uprooted alder or willow. Mazeppa's Ukraine stallion, or the mightiest *destrier* that ever

Paladin bestrode, would have been whirled away like withered leaves, ere they had swam ten of the seven hundred yards that lay between us and the Virginian shore. I could hardly believe my eyes when Hoyle pointed out to me the fording-place where, on the 23rd of last December, he had crossed without wetting his horse's girth.

It was waste of time to look longer, so, in no pleasant mood, I returned to the farm-house, and a council of war was incontinently held. The Marylanders had already arranged their plan; they had a vague idea of some ferry to the Northward, and intended to grope their way to it somehow. Before attempting this it was necessary to divest themselves of any suspicious articles, either of baggage or accoutrement; indeed, they left every scrap of clothing behind, except what they carried on their persons, and one change of under-raiment sewn up in the folds of a rug. They meant to assume the character of small cattle-dealers, and, as far as appearance went, succeeded perfectly—nothing more unmilitary can be conceived. Their horses were possibly hardy and active, but stunted, mean-looking animals, while the saddle-gear would have been dear, anywhere, at five dollars. The men themselves had the lazy, slouching look, peculiar to the hybrid class with which they wished to be identified. They were civil and sorry enough about the turn affairs had taken; but evidently quite determined that we

should part company. The elder of the two took
me aside, and spoke thus, as near as I can remember,—

"Look ye, Major, I'm right-down sorry about
this here; and I'd have liked well to have gone slick
through with ye, but it won't work in the parts we're
agoing to try. Four men and horses ain't so easy put
up as two, and there ain't many as'll venture it.
The sort o' your brown horse is kind'er uncommon
up along there; they'd spot *him* if they didn't
spot you, and you'd never get to look like a citizen,—
not if you was to shave and wear a wig. There's no
two words about it : it ain't to be done."

I believe the man intended to gild the pill with a
rough compliment : in any case I was bound to
swallow it. There was no sort of contract between
us, nor any promise of remuneration ; I only rode by
sufferance in that company. I felt, too, that he was
right : it would be very difficult for any Englishman—
drilled or undrilled—to disguise himself as a Virginian
cattle-dealer, so that keen native eyes could not detect
the *travestie*. I do not think I should have pressed
the point, even had I been in a position to do so ; as
it was, I yielded with good grace, only begging my
late companions to let me have the earliest information as to the route, if they succceeded in getting
through. This they readily promised ; so, with
the concurrence of the good Walter, I determined to
fall back, for the present, on my original 'base,'

with the consoling reflection, that I was only imitating
the most renowned Federal commanders.

All this was scarcely settled, when our host hurried
in—rather a blank look on his bold face—to say
that one of his contrabands had just come in, after
an absence of two hours : he had taken one of his
master's horses without leave, and absolutely declined
to state where, or why, he had gone. As 1800
Federals, including a regiment of cavalry, occupied
Poolesville—only six miles off—it was easy to guess
in what direction the truant had wandered. There
was no time for argument; even chastisement was
reserved for a more fitting season : in fifteen minutes
more, we had ridden swiftly across the cleared
lands, and, with Hoyle for our pilot, were winding
through the ravines and glades of the White Grounds.
The day was dull and cloudy ; so, having no sun to
guide us, we, the strangers, speedily lost all idea of
direction ; even Walter, the confident, owned himself
fairly puzzled. But our host led on at a steady pace,
never pausing to consult landmarks or memory ;
evidently every bush and brake was familiar to him ;
there was not the ghost of a track, but we seemed
generally to follow the winding of a rapid shallow
stream, up whose channel we often scrambled for forty
yards or more.

> We hadna ridden a league, a league,
> O' leagues but barely three,

when we struck a path leading straight through the

H

woods to Clarksburg—the first point on the proposed route of the two Marylanders : they meant to feel their way, cautiously, thence in a north-westerly direction ; the elder had one or two acquaintances in the neighbourhood of Frederick City that he hoped would assist them. So, with leave-takings, hurried but amicable, our party separated. We, the other three, proposed to make for our quarters of the last Sunday, and for ten miles further our kind host rode in our company, absolutely refusing to turn back till we were in a country that Walter knew right well, and might be considered comparatively safe : then he left us, proposing to return home by another and yet more circuitous route, so as to baffle possible pursuers. He did get home safe, but was arrested within the same week,—not, I trust, before he had moderately chastised that treacherous contraband—and we met, two months later, in the Old Capitol.

Three hours' more riding brought us within sight of the farm, where we intended to refresh ourselves and our cattle, and, perhaps, to abide for the night. We relied so implicitly on the hospitality we were certain to find, that we had provided ourselves with no food of any sort : my flask, too, had been emptied on the previous night. Fancy our disgust, when we found the shutters closed, everything carefully locked up, and no living soul about the place but two helpless little coloured persons of tender age. The whole family had gone out to a sledging ' frolic,' and would

not return till late at night; it was then past 5 p.m.;
we had breakfasted lightly at seven, and been in
the saddle ever since nine o'clock. We did discover
some Indian corn for the horses, and left them to feed
under their old shed, only removing bridles and
loosening girths.

About ten minutes later, we were sitting under
the house-porch—it was narrow and deep, as is the
fashion in those parts, and boarded up the sides
breast-high; I was lighting a sullen pipe, hoping to
deaden the hungry cravings which could not be satisfied, when I felt my arm pulled violently; a hoarse
whisper said in my ear,—" By G—d, they've got us,"
—turning, I met the good Walter's face, white and
convulsed with emotions which I care not to define
or remember. Alick was already crouching below
the boarding, and I stooped too, mechanically; as I
did so, I followed the direction of the guide's haggard
eyes. By my faith, just where the wood opened on
the clearing, about 180 yards to our front, there sat
on their horses six Federal dragoons, surveying the
landscape with some interest. It was very odd to see
them gazing straight down upon us, evidently unconscious of our proximity; but they were looking from
light into the shadow of the porch: fortunately, too,
the horses were well under cover. It chanced that,
close to the gate in the outermost enclosure, there
was a watering-pond; around and from this, tracks
of all kinds of cattle crossed and diverged in every

direction : as we entered we had remarked many hoof-
prints turning abruptly to the right, probably left by
the sleighing party. The dragoons halted five minutes
or so in consultation ; then they turned and rode off
quickly along that same right-hand track. The house
was so evidently shut up, that I presume they thought
it would be wasted time if they searched it then.

Resistance would have been utterly out of the
question, even if the numbers had been more equal,
for the only arms in the party were my own—a long
hunting-knife worn in my belt, and a five-shooter
carried by Alick: so we prepared for escape instantly.
I had to go round to the back of the house to get my
hunting-crop, which I had left there. When I came
out I found Walter already mounted : his mare was
not in the same shed with our horses. In a few hurried words, he explained that it would be best for *him*
to make off at once, and wait for us in the woods
below, to which the clearing sloped down from the
homestead. Though I had before formed my own
opinion as to his vaunted valiance, I confess I was
rather disappointed ; but he was not a hireling,
and I had no right to prevent him looking after
his own safety first ; I only shrugged my shoulders
without replying, and went into the other shed to
help Alick saddle up. The Alabamian was much
less delicate or more determined than myself : when
he heard of Walter's intentions, his face darkened
threateningly.

" By the ——— ! " he said, " he ain't going to quit after that fashion ; " and, as he went out towards the corner where Walter still lingered, I saw his hand shift back to the butt of my revolver. Now, I was too sensible of the guide's good intentions and disinterested kindness, to wish to press hardly on a temporary loss of nerve : so I busied myself with buckle and curb-link, and refrained from assisting at the debate : it was very brief, nor can I say if Alick's arguments were intimidating or conciliatory ; I rather suspected the former, from the expression of his face when he returned, simply remarking : " I've made it all right, Major. He stops with us as long as we want him to."

Ten minutes afterwards we gained the shelter of the woods, and, keeping always well down in the gullies or hollows, were picking our way in a direction nearly parallel to that taken by our pursuers. This was our only course, as we dared not show ourselves as yet across open ground or along travelled roads. We might have ridden about a league and a half—it is difficult to judge distance in thick cover and over broken ground, with pace constantly varied—when our guide's confidence returned, and, with it, his weakness for self-laudation. He began once more to recount his many narrow escapes, and was sanguine as to his chance of pulling through this— the closest shave of all. We were halting on the bank of a muddy, swollen stream, in some doubt whether we should try the treacherous bottom there or higher up, when, looking over my shoulder, I saw the figures of four horsemen, looming large against the red evening sky as they passed slowly across the sky-line, on the crest of some abrupt rising ground about 300 yards to our right : soon two more showed themselves, making the pursuing party complete ; they were evidently retracing their steps—for what reason I know not. Almost at the same instant the Alabamian caught sight of the enemy ; but before he could speak I touched our guide on the shoulder with my hunting-whip, pointing in the direction of the danger. If you ever saw a wing-tipped mallard's flurry when the retriever comes upon him unawares, you will have a good idea of how the valiant Walter ' squattered ' through the ford. The twilight was darkening fast, and, in the shadow of the ravine, we were almost safe from the eyes of our pursuers ; but I marvel that even at such a distance their ears were not attracted by the flounder and the splash. My squire and I followed more leisurely ; indeed, throughout, the former had displayed a creditable coolness and determination : also, he seemed to take very kindly to my own favourite motto, *Festina lente*—More haste, worse speed.

That was our last look at the dragoons. We learnt afterwards that, later in the evening, they searched the farmhouse (the family had just returned), and not only struck our trail through the woods, but held it within three miles of our resting-place for the night ; there the numerous cross roads, and the utter confusion of many tracks, baffled our pursuers ; probably too, their horses by that time were in poor condition for following up an indefinite chase.

Alick and I determined to push for our original starting-point—the house of Symonds of that ilk. Another two hours' riding brought us to where a lane turned off towards Bon Gualtier's home. He was evidently anxious to find himself a free agent ; this time, even the Alabamian did not seek to detain him. The rest of the road we had traversed, on the preceding Saturday, and we could hardly miss our way. So there I parted from my honest guide, with many kind wishes on his side, and hearty thanks on mine. I rather repent having alluded to that little nervousness : but, after all, it was hardly a question of physical courage ; we sought to avoid imprisonment, not peril to life or limb.

My stout horse, Falcon, strode cheerily over the last of those dark, tiresome miles without a stumble or sign of weariness ; but the roan's ears were drooping, and he slouched along heavily on his shoulders long before we saw the lights of Symonds' homestead, where we met a hearty, if not joyful welcome. We had not tasted food for thirteen hours, during which we had scarcely been out of the saddle ; so even disappointment could not prevent our relish-

ing to the uttermost the savoury supper with which
our hostess would fain have comforted us.

Our talk was chiefly of the future, about which
Symonds did not despond, though he was disposed
to blame, somewhat sharply, our late companions, for
choosing to find their way South independently; I
thought he was unjust then, and since, I have had
ample evidence of their good intentions and good
faith.

The next morning I rode Falcon down into Baltimore, there to await fresh tidings, leaving Alick and
the roan at Symonds', to await fresh orders.

CHAPTER VI.

THE FERRY.

I HAD not been in Baltimore three days when my plans were somewhat altered by the introduction of a fresh agent. The guide, who accompanied Lord Hartington and Colonel Leslie, had returned unexpectedly, and Symonds pressed me strongly to secure his services. He had made the traverse several times successfully, and was thoroughly acquainted with most of the ground on both banks of the Potomac. He had now made his way on foot from the Shenandoah Valley, across the Alleghany Range, to Oakland; thence by the cars to somewhere near Sykesville, on the Baltimore and Ohio Railroad. Here, the day began to break, and he would not trust farther to the short-sightedness of Federal officials; so he looked out for a soft place in a snow-drift, and leapt out, alighting without injury. The same reasons that made reticence useless in Hoyle's case apply here : to both men Republican justice has done its worst long ago. My new guide's name was Shipley. He was lying *perdu* in Baltimore when I first heard of him, so there was no difficulty in arranging an interview.

After some hesitation, and not a little negotiation, Shipley agreed to pilot me through by one route or another. He was to ride my second horse, and keep the animal as a remuneration for his services, so soon as we should be fairly within Confederate lines. He would not promise to start before the expiration of a full week, as the clothes and other necessaries which he had come specially to obtain could not be got ready sooner. This new arrangement involved two changes which did not please me, viz., the elimination of poor Alick from the party, and the shifting of my saddlebags from the roan on to Falcon, for the guide stipulated that each should carry his own baggage. Symonds, however, was very urgent that I should close with the conditions at once; he had the highest opinion of Shipley's talents and trustworthiness, and insisted that such a chance should not be let slip. He promised that Alick, if possible, should be provided with a mount, so as to be still enabled to accompany us. *I* could not, of course, be expected to increase my already double risk in horse-flesh.

So we struck hands on the bargain, and I resigned myself pretty contentedly to another delay. The days passed rapidly, as they always did in Baltimore. On most afternoons I rode Falcon out for exercise and ' schooling.' He soon became very clever at the only obstacles you encounter in crossing this country —timber fences, and small brooks with steep broken banks; though, to the last, he always would hang a little in taking off, he never dreamt of refusing.

Before the week was quite out, Alick came down from Symonds', bringing tidings of our late companions, the two Marylanders. They had succeeded in crossing by a horse-ferry at Shepherdstown—a small village not far from Sharpsburg, and about seven miles from the battle-field of Antietam. The letter was written from the south bank of the Potomac, and furnished us with all the necessary names and halting-points on the route. Now, everything looked promising again. It was soon settled that Alick and Shipley should make their way across the country to Sharpsburg with the two horses: this was the latter's own arrangement, and *he*, too, was unkind enough to object to my un-citizenlike appearance. I was to meet them there, at a certain house, on a certain day, travelling by another route—through Frederick City.

Thither I betook myself by the train leaving Baltimore, on the afternoon of March the 10th, arriving at Frederick nearly two hours behind time, in consequence of a difficulty between the wheels and the rails, the latter having become sulkily slippery with the sleet that came on in earnest after nightfall. Very early the next morning I started for Petersville, near which village, in the shadow of the South Mountain, lay the country-house of the good-natured friend who had offered to forward me to Sharpsburg.

I shall not easily forget that drive; the distance
was rather under fourteen miles, and it was performed in something over four hours; yet the load
consisted simply of my driver, myself, and my saddle-
bags, in the lightest conceivable waggon, drawn by
a pair of horses specially selected for strength rather
than speed. We travelled on a broad turnpike, not
inferior, I was told, in ordinary times to the average
of such roads; in many places the mud literally
touched the axles, and more than once we should
have been set fast in spite of the struggles of our
team, if I had not lightened the weight by descending
into a quagmire that reached fully half-way up my
thigh-boots.

At last we struggled through, reaching my friend's
house with no other damage than some strained
spokes and a broken spring. There I found horses
ready caparisoned, and a faithful contraband to guide
me on my way. The ride was as pleasant as the
drive had been disagreeable. It was positive rest, to
exchange the jolting and jerking of the carriage for
the familiar sway of the saddle. I had a strong
hackney under me, a bright clear sky overhead, and
a companion who, if not brilliantly amusing, was
very passably intelligent. He was able to tell me all
about the South Mountain fight; indeed, our route
lay right across the centre of that bloody battle-
ground. Riding along the valley with the hills on
our left we soon came to Birkettsville: close above

was the scene of the most furious assaults, and the
most obstinate struggle. The quaint little hamlet—
reminding you of a Dutch village—looked cheerful
enough now, as the sun shimmered over the dark-
red bricks, and glistening roofs grouped round a
more glittering chapel-cupola; yet one could not
help remembering, that thither, on a certain afternoon, in just such pleasant weather, maimed men
by hundreds, crawled or were carried in; and
that for weeks after, scarce one of those cozy houses
but sheltered some miserable being moaning his
tortured life away. The undulating champaign
between the Catoctin and South Mountains, that
forms the broad Middletown valley, seems to invite the
manœuvres of infantry battalions; but, climbing the
steep ascent in the teeth of musketry and field-
batteries, must have been sharp work. Indeed,
though the assailing force doubtless far outnumbered
the defenders, I think the carrying of those heights
one of the most creditable achievements in the
War.

The terrible handwriting of the God of Battles is
still very plainly to be discerned; all along the moun-
tain-side, trees—bent, blasted, and broken—tell where
round-shot or grape tore through; and scored bark,
closing often over imbedded bullets, shows where
beat most stormily the leaden hail. Near the crest
of the mountain, there are several patches of ground,
utterly differing in colour from the soil around, and

evidently recently disturbed. You want no guide to tell you that in those Golgothas moulder corpses by hundreds, cast in pell-mell, with scanty rites of sepulture. Beside these common trenches, there are always some single graves, occasionally marked by a post with initials roughly carved. It is good to see that, after the bitter fight, some were found, not so weary or so hurried, but that they could find time to do a dead comrade—perhaps even a dead enemy— one last kindness.

Descending from the ridge, we rode some way up a narrow valley—where overhanging pine-woods, and soft green pastures, traversed by rapid streams, re- minded me often of the Ardennes—and then climbed the Elk Range, beyond which lies the field of Antie- tam. We soon crossed the Creek, along whose banks was waged the fierce battle, that made men think as lightly of the South Mountain fight as if it had been but a passing skirmish; and I rode up to the ap- pointed meeting-place in Sharpsburg, a few minutes in advance of the appointed hour.

My first question, after making myself known to the goodman of the house, was, naturally, of my horses and men. Will you be kind enough to fancy my feelings, when I heard that they were miles away, and—the reason why? Three days before, the ferry- boat had been carried away and shattered by the floods; nothing but a skiff could cross till a cable was rigged from bank to bank; there was no chance

of this being completed before the beginning of the
following week. The neighbourhood was too dangerous to linger in; there was a provost-marshal
guard actually stationed in Sharpsburg: so my
men, hearing of the disaster on their road, had
very properly remained at their last halting-place,
about ten miles farther up the country. I was so
savagely disappointed that I hardly listened to my
new friend, as he proceeded to give some useful hints
on our route and conduct, whenever we should succeed in getting over the river. I only remember one
suggestion—'if I was stopped anywhere this side of
Winchester, I might give a fictitious name, and say
that I was going to visit *my son*, an officer in the
Federal army.' Now, as I have barely entered on
my eighth lustre, I can only suppose that the great
bitterness of my heart imparted to my face, for the
moment, a helpless — perhaps imbecile — look of
senility. I had no alternative, however, but to retreat, as my men had done; the place was evidently
too hot to hold me : already, through the window, I
saw a shabby dragoon paying suspicious attention
to my horses, contraband, and saddlebags. I was
greatly relieved, on going out, to find that the warrior
was too stupidly drunk to be actuated by anything
beyond an idle, purposeless curiosity. So, after
receiving directions as to where I was likely to rejoin
my companions, I set my face north-east again, and
rode out into the deepening darkness with feelings

not much less sullen than the black rack of clouds
massed up behind, that broke upon us, right soon,
with wind and drenching rain.

My horse, as well as I, must have been glad
when we reached the homestead we were seeking;
for throughout the afternoon I had ridden quickly
wherever there was level ground, calculating on a
night's rest in Sharpsburg. I had some difficulty in
convincing the farmer that I was a true man and no
spy ; having once realised the fact, he showed himself
not less hospitable than his fellows. I was not surprised to find my men gone ; with all his goodwill to
the cause, their host had not dared to entertain such
suspicious strangers longer than twenty-four hours ;
for keen eyes and ready tongues were rife all round,
(we had proof already, in poor George Hoyle's case,
how quickly and sternly the charge of 'harbouring
disaffected persons' could be acted upon :) he had
sent the men to separate secluded farmhouses, whence
they could be summoned at a few hours' warning.
He strongly advised me to wait elsewhere till the
horse-ferry was re-established, of which he promised
to give me the very earliest intelligence : so I at once
determined to take the Hagerstown stage to Frederick next morning (the house stood not many yards
from the main road), and the rail from thence back
to Baltimore, leaving men and horses in their present
quarters. It was evident that the honest Irishman
(he was an emigrant of twenty years' standing) spoke

thus in perfect sincerity, from no lack of hospitality. Though in poor mood for conviviality, I did strive hard, all that evening, to meet his social overtures half way; simply that I might not appear ungracious or ungrateful.

The homestead nestles close to the foot of the South Mountain, near Middletown Gap, some miles north of the point where I had crossed that day. We talked, of course, about the battles (they were within sound, though not sight, of Antietam). I found that a field-hospital had been established in the field immediately adjoining the orchard, and that some of the wounded, chiefly Confederates, who could not be moved, had lain there for many days. I asked the goodwife how she felt while the Southern armament was marching past her doors.

"Well," she said, "I wasn't greatly skeared; only I thought I'd pull down the new parlour-curtains; but they behaved right well, and didn't meddle with nothin' to signify; not like them Yankees, who are always pickin' and stealin'. But I'd like to get right out of this country, anyhow; we'll never do no good here while the war lasts."

I wonder how many voices, if they dared speak out, would join in the dreary *refrain* of those last few words?

No noteworthy incident marked my journey back to Baltimore. I remained there till the following Tuesday, and, in that interval, received a note from

Shipley, which both puzzled and disquieted me : it was purposely vague and obscure; but, as far as I could make out, the writer thought it would be better at once to make for some point north-west of Cumberland—to retrace, in fact, the route that he had himself recently traversed; I rather inferred that he meant to move in that direction without waiting for me, leaving me to make my way to a rendezvous which he would appoint by letter. Now, of all parties concerned in the expedition, the one whose safety I valued next to my own was—Falcon. I had been loth to trust him, even so far, to a rider about whose qualifications I knew nothing,—except that it was very unlikely he would have good 'hands;' and had no notion of risking the good horse, without me, on an indefinitely long journey, where he might be indifferently cared for. I wrote at once to stop any such movement; and with this I was forced to be content.

Late on the Monday evening the expected summons reached me—sent specially by train. The next morning I started for Frederick, whence I intended to drive through Middletown to Boonesborough, near which was the place of meeting. The first thing I saw in the morning paper, which I began to read in the cars, was a fresh general order, suggestive of most unpleasant misgivings. General Kelly had just succeeded to the command of Maryland Heights, and of the Division specially selected for picket duty on the river. This—his first order—enjoined the seizure of all boats of every description between Monocacy Creek and St. John's (comprising the whole of the Upper Potomac) : no passenger or merchandise could be conveyed from Maryland into Virginia without a proper pass, and then only at two specified places —Harper's Ferry and Point of Rocks : any one transgressing this edict was liable to arrest and trial by martial law.

Throwing down the ill-omened journal, I could not forbear a muttered quotation : ' The day looks dark for England.' Nevertheless, I drove on straight from Frederick, determined to prove what the morrow would bring forth. It was late when we reached the small road-side hotel, on the ridge of the South Mountain, where I had arranged to halt for the night; but, late as it was, I had time to hear fresh evil tidings before I slept.

The Shepherdstown ferry was in working order at noon on the Monday. The same evening, soon after dusk, four mounted men, with two led horses, rode down, requiring to be set across instantly. The ferryman objected, stating that his orders were imperative against putting any one over, after sundown, without a special pass. The men insisted, stating that they bore despatches from Kelly to Milroy, and enforced their demands with threats. The unhappy ferryman was absolutely unarmed, and only wished to escape. They shot him to death without further parley, under the eyes of his mother

and sister, who saw all from their windows. Then
they ferried themselves and their horses across, and
left the boat on the Virginian bank, after knocking
out two or three of her planks.   Naturally there was
a great revulsion of popular feeling in the country,
and there had been a real *émeute* round the murdered
man's grave, when they buried him, that day, in
Sharpsburg: no one, suspected of Southern sympathies,
could venture openly to appear.   From all I could
learn, the authors of that butchery were not Confederate soldiers, or even guerillas, but purely and
simply horse-thieves, who had come over with the
sole object of plunder, tempted by the enormous
prices that horse-flesh could then command in
Virginia.

Very early the next morning I had a visit from the
Irishman, who lived hard by.   Things did not look
less gloomy when I had heard what he had to tell.
To begin with, that unlucky tongue of Alick's had been
doing all sorts of mischief.   He never touched strong
liquors, so there was not even that excuse for his imprudence.   Instead of remaining quiet in the secluded
retreat to which he had been sent, he would persist
in hanging about in the immediate neighbourhood of
Boonesborough, and appeared to have spoken freely
about our projects, greatly exalting and exaggerating
their importance ; indeed, he could scarcely have said
more if we had been travelling as accredited agents
between two belligerent Powers.   Such garrulity

was not only intensely provoking, but involved
real peril to all parties concerned. I thought
the Irishman was thoroughly right in taking that
blundering bull by the horns, and acting decisively
on his own responsibility, inasmuch as there was no
time to communicate with me. He insisted that the
Alabamian should quit the neighbourhood without an
hour's delay,—there had already been talk of his
arrest,—furnishing him with certain necessaries and
a few dollars on my account. In despite of the edict
aforesaid, there were still punts and skiffs concealed
all along the river bank, and a footman unincum-
bered with baggage could always be put over without
difficulty. Indeed, Alick had actually crossed into
Virginia, and returned safely, while he was loitering
about Boonesborough. I never saw the Alabamian
again : he carried away with him my best wishes and
my revolver, and I hope they have profited him.
Where caution or diplomacy are not required, his
sterling honesty and dogged courage will always
stand him and others in good stead ; if his superiors
can only tie up his tongue, I believe they will 'make
a man of him yet.'

As to Shipley, I found that it was not considered
prudent for him to await my arrival there, for a search
might be made over the Irishman's premises at any
moment. He had been sent back, on the previous
afternoon, to a house near Newmarket, a village some
thirty miles east of Boonesborough, so that we must

almost have crossed on the high road leading to
Frederick City ; there, I was certain to find both him
and Falcon.

The Irishman was decidedly of opinion that to
persevere in our enterprise at the Shepherdstown
ferry, or anywhere in the immediate neighbourhood,
would be not only the height of rashness, but absolute
waste of time.   He advised our striking northward
at once, by the Cumberland route, which then appeared to be the only one offering possible chances of
success.   Even on the Lower Potomac, the *cordon* of
pickets and guard-boats had been so strengthened of
late as to become well-nigh impervious, and captures
were of hourly occurrence.

Slowly—and I fear rather sullenly—I admitted the
justice of my friend's counsel, as I walked down to
his stable, where the roan had been standing since
Alick's departure.

Perhaps even while I write, the war-tide is surging
backwards and forwards once again past the doors
of that cozy homestead ; but I trust its roof-tree is
still inviolate by fire or sword, and that no rude
hand has scorched or torn the 'new parlour cur-
tains,' in which my trim little hostess took an
innocent pride.

It was past noon when I bade farewell to my friends,
and mounted the roan, to strike Shipley's back-trail.
There was a bright blue sky overhead, though the wind
blew intensely cold, and hoofs on the hard-frozen

ground rang, as on pavement. For the first eighteen miles or so, which brought us to Frederick, my horse stepped out cheerily enough, though he carried far more weight than he had yet been burdened with, in the shape of myself and full saddlebags. Here we baited, at an obscure inn which had been recommended to me as 'safe;' and late in the afternoon held on for Newmarket. I found the farm-house I sought without any difficulty, but the owner was down in the village, a mile or so off. Without dismounting, I asked to see the mistress, and a thin, sickly-looking woman came to the door. At my first question—relating of course to Shipley—a glimmer of distrust dawned on her vague, white face—"There was no one there except their own family, and she had never seen or heard of a man on a brown horse." I was too thoroughly inured to disappointment by this time to feel angry—much less surprised—at anything in that line. Evidently I had to do with one of those impracticable yet timorous females—strong in their very weakness—who will persist in bearing a meek false-witness till the examiner's patience fails. So my answer was quiet enough.

"Pardon me, I think your memory is treacherous. You surely must, at least once in your natural life, have seen or heard of 'a man on a brown horse.' But if you have known nothing of such a remarkable pair within—the last month for instance, I fear you can't help me much. If you will tell me where to find your

husband in Newmarket, and allow me to light my pipe,
I'll not trouble you any more."

These benevolences the pale woman did not withhold;
but she saw me depart with a wintry smile, and I heard
her distinctly mutter to a handmaiden—fearfully arid
and adust—who peered over her mistress's shoulder,

"There's another on 'em, *I* know."

I found the husband in Newmarket, easily enough—
at the 'store,' of course : this is invariably the centre
of all gossiping and liquoring-up, in such villages as
cannot boast a public bar-room.   When I delivered
certain verbal credentials, he was disposed to be more
communicative than his spouse; but his information
was not very clear or satisfactory.   It appeared that
on the previous morning, some hour before dawn, a
man had knocked at the door and asked for shelter :
from the description, I at once recognised my guide
and Falcon.   For once, Shipley's over-caution told
against him : he not only declined to give his name,
but would not state, precisely, whence he came or
whither he was going : there were many Federal
spies about, laying traps for Southern sympathisers;
so the farmer got suspicious, and, instead of wel-
coming the stranger, prayed him to pass on his
way.   This solitary instance of inhospitality is thus
easily accounted for.   I could not blame my informant; but the state of things was enough to chafe
even a meek temper : the roan's long legs had
begun to tire under the unwonted weight before

I reached Newmarket, and he rolled fearfully in the slowest trot. Yet I had sworn not to sleep before I laid my hand on Falcon's mane, and I felt, with every fresh check, more savagely determined to keep the trail, as long as horse-flesh would last. I knew there were few places in that country where Shipley would dare to trust himself even for a night's lodging: some of his relations lived within half a league of Symonds; if he meant fairly by me and mine, he was certain to advise the latter of his return: so I resolved to push straight on for my old quarters. Between me and the wished-for *gîte* there lay sixteen miles of hilly road—darkling every minute faster.

I do not care to remember that dreary ride—or rather, walk—for two thirds of the distance were done on foot. For awhile I had pleasanter companions than my own sullen thoughts: a pair of blue-birds kept with me, for two or three miles at least, fluttering and twittering along the fences by my side, with the prettiest sociability—sometimes ahead, sometimes behind—never more than a dozen yards off; their brilliant plumage gleaming through the twilight like jets of sapphire flame: I felt absurdly sorry when they disappeared at last into the deepening blackness. I had been warned of the probability of encountering a cavalry picket somewhere on my road: so I was not greatly surprised when the possible peril became a certain one. I was riding slowly up

a low, steep hill, about ten miles from Newmarket
(I think the two or three houses are dignified by the
name of Rockville), when I saw the indistinct forms
of several horses, and the taller figure of one
mounted man, standing out against the clear night-
sky on the very crest of the ascent. I drew rein
instinctively; but in that particular frame of mind,
I don't think I should have turned back, if the gates
of the Old Capitol had stood open across the road.
So I jogged steadily on, trying to look as innocently
unconscious as possible. Seven or eight horses were
picketed to some posts outside what I conclude was
a whisky-store; the troopers were all comforting
themselves within; the intense cold had probably
made the solitary sentinel drowsy, for his head
drooped low on his breast, and he never lifted it
as I rode past. I could not attempt to make a run
of it, so I did not quicken my speed, when the
danger was left behind: indeed I halted more than
once, listening for the sound of hoofs in my rear, in
which case I should have plunged into the black
woods on either side, so as to let the pursuit pass
by. Hearing nothing, I dismounted again, and
strode on rather more cheerfully.

The roan was not more glad than his rider, when
we groped our way up the lane, leading through
fields to Symonds' homestead. The goodwife came
out quickly, in answer to my hail, her husband being
absent, as usual.

" Oh, Major," she said, " I can't say how glad I am to see you. Shipley's so anxious about you: he hasn't been gone half-an-hour."

" And the brown horse "—I broke in.

" He's in the stable; and looking right well."

With a huge sigh of relief, I flung myself out of the saddle.

" That'll do, Mrs. Symonds. I don't want to hear another word, unless it relates to—ham and eggs."

Truly, I fear that the neat-handed Phillis must have been aweary, that night, before she had satisfied Gargantua. A messenger soon summoned Shipley, and he was with me before midnight: he explained all his movements satisfactorily, and I could not but acknowledge he had acted throughout discreetly and well. We sate far into the morning, discussing future plans. Ultimately it was settled, that he should start with the roan, so soon as the animal should be rested and fit for the road, travelling by moderate stages to some meeting-place near Oakland. The rendezvous was to be determined by information he would receive in those parts; and I was to be advised of it by a letter left for me in Cumberland. Shipley reckoned that it would take him ten days at least to make his point. That interval I was to spend in Baltimore; from which I was to proceed, with my horse, to Cumberland, in the cars. This plan had the double advantage of saving Falcon over

200 miles of march, and of enabling my guide to make his way, more securely, as a solitary traveller. He could not trust himself on the railroad, nor would it have been safe to attempt the transport of two horses.

So, on the following day, I made—anything but a triumphant—entry into Baltimore.   Kindly greetings and condolences could not enable me during that last visit to shake off a restless discontent—a dark distrust of the future—a vague sense of shameful defeat.

CHAPTER VII.

EARLY on Monday the 30th of April, I addressed myself to the journey once more, taking the cars to Cumberland, whither Falcon had preceded me by two days, and this time I bound myself by a vow—not lightly to be broken—that I would not see Baltimore again, of free will or free agency, till I had heard the tuck of Southern drums.

The most remarkable part of the road is from Point of Rocks to Harper's Ferry, inclusive, where the rails find a narrow space to creep between the river and the cliffs of Catoctin and Elk Mountains. The last-named spot is especially picturesque; standing on a promontory washed on either side by the Potomac and Shenandoah, with all the natural advantages of abrupt rocks, feathery hanging woods and broken water. Thenceforward there is little to interest, or to compensate for the sluggishness of pace and frequency of delays. The track winds on always through the same monotony of forest and hill; plunging into the gorges and climbing the shoulders of bluffs, with the audacity of gradient and contempt of curve that marks the handiwork of

American engineers. I wonder that one of these did not take Mount Cenis in hand, and save the monster tunnel. The line was strongly picketed; everywhere you saw the same fringe of murky-white tents, and at every station the same groups of squalid soldiery.

What especially exasperated *me* was, the incessant and continuous neighbourhood of the Potomac; if you left it for a few minutes you were certain to come upon it again, before the eye had time to forget the everlasting foam-splashed ochre of the sullen current; at each fresh point it met you undiminished in volume, unabated in turbulency. Long before this, I had begun to look at the river in the light of a personal enemy. I think that Xerxes in the matter of the Hydaspes* did wisely and well. With his resources of men and money, I would fain do so and more likewise to that same Potomac—subdividing its waters, till the pet spaniel of 'my Mary Jane' should ford them without wetting the silky fringes of her trailing ears.

Theoretically, a road passing through leagues of forest-clad hills ought to be pleasant, if not interesting; practically, you are bored to death before you get half-way through. There is a remarkable scarcity of anything like fine-grown timber: the underwood is luxuriant enough, especially where the mountain laurel abounds; but in ten thousand acres of stunted firwood, you would look in vain for any one tree fit

* I quote from memory here, and am rather vague about nomenclature.

to compare with the grey giants that watch over Nor-
wegian fiords, or fit to rank in ' the shadowy army of
the Unterwalden pines.'

We reached Cumberland shortly after sundown;
my first visit was to the stables where I hoped to
find Falcon. Imagine my disgust on hearing that,
through an accident on the line, the unlucky horse
had been shut up for forty-six hours in his box, with
provender just enough for one day. He had been
well tended, however, and judiciously fed in small
quantities at frequent intervals, and, barring that he
looked rather 'tucked up,' did not seem much the
worse for his enforced fast.

I found Shipley's letter, too, where I had been told
to expect it; he had got so far without let or hindrance; the meeting-place was set about forty miles
north-west of Cumberland. I spent the evening, not
unpleasantly, partly at the house of a ' sympathising '
resident to whom I had been recommended; partly
in the society of the most miraculous Milesian I ever
encountered—off the stage or out of a book. No pen
could reproduce the torrent of his turgid eloquence;
no pencil could do justice to his grotesque mobility
of feature or to his unctuous wealth of far-flowing
hair, while before his magnificent brogue orthogra-
phic audacity quails. He was stationed in Cumberland on some sort of recruiting service, and,
from dawn to midnight, never ceased to oil his
already lissome tongue with ' caulkers ' of every

imaginable liquor.   I was told that at no hour of
the twenty-four had any man seen him thoroughly
drunk or decently sober.   When we first met, his
cups had brought him nearly to the end of the belligerent or irascible stage; he was then inveighing
against the dwellers in the Shenandoah Valley, where
he had lately been quartered, for their want of
patriotism in declining to furnish their defenders (?)
with gratuitous whisky and tobacco ; threatening the
most dreadful reprisals, when he should visit 'thim
desateful Copperhids' again.   Suddenly, without
warning, he slid into the maudlin phase; taking up
his parable of lamentation against 'this crule warr.'

   " I weep, sirr," said he, " over the rrupture of mee
adhopted counthree—the counthreé that resaved me
with opin arrums, when I was floying from the feece
of toyrants," &c., &c.

   When he informed me that he belonged to Mulligan's division, the words—" I suppose so "—escaped
me, involuntarily.   Truly, if the rest of the brigade
resembled the specimen before me, only the mighty
Celt, whom Thackeray had made immortal, could fitly
command it.   I shall never again look on the 'stock'
Irishman as an exaggeration or caricature.

   I waited, the next morning, till a heavy snow-storm
had resolved itself into a thin, driving sleet; then my
saddlebags were strapped on Falcon, and I set forth
alone ; the good horse striding away, as strong under
me as if he had never heard of short commons.   We

baited at Frostburgh, a small village set on a hill
mined and tunnelled with coal-pits; fifteen miles or
so beyond this was the roadside inn where I proposed
to halt for the night. The sun had long set when I
rode up to a spectral-looking white house; remarking, with no pleasant surprise, that not a vestige of
smoke rose from its gaunt chimneys. At the gate
there stood a cart laden with some sort of household
goods; near this, a man, who lounged up, seeing
me draw rein, to ask my business. It appeared that
a 'flitting' had taken place that very day, and that
he, the goodman, was then betaking himself, with
the residue of the chattels, to their new home, about
five miles back on the Frostburgh road, whither his
family had already gone. The next chance of a billet
was at Grantsville, two leagues farther on. Now that
sounds too absurdly short a distance to disquiet any
traveller; but neither is the fatal straw in the camel's
load a ponderous thing, *per se*. Both Falcon and I had
reckoned that our day's work was done when we
climbed the last hill; so it was in some discontent that
we set our faces once more against the black road,
and the stinging sleet, and the bitter north wind.

Amongst Mrs. Browning's earlier poems, there is
one, to my mind almost peerless, for sweet sonority of
verse-music and simplicity of strength. If it chance
that any reader of mine has not encountered 'The
Rhyme of the Duchess May,' this page, at least, has
not been written in vain. My saddle-bags held no

K

volume other than a note-book; but that ballad in
manuscript was nearly the last gift bestowed on me
in Baltimore. Never was mortal mood less romantic
than mine; so, I cannot account for the fancy which
impelled me, there and then, to recite aloud, how—

> The bridegroom led the flight, on his red roan steed of might;
> And the bride lay on his arm, still, as tho' she feared no harm,
>   Smiling out into the night.
>
> "Fearest thou?" he said at last.   "Nay," she answered him in
>   haste,
> "Not such death as we could find; only life with one behind,
>   Ride on—fast as fear—ride fast."

I found one listener, more appreciative than the
wild pine-barren, that surely had never been waked
by rhythmic sound since the birthday of Time. Falcon
pricked his ears, and champed his bit cheerily, while
he mended his pace without warning of spur. As for
myself—the pure, earnest Saxon diction proved a
more efficient 'comforter' than the many-coloured
scarf round my neck, wrought by the same kind
'white hands beyond the sea;' hands that, even
now, I venture to salute with the lips of a grateful
spirit, in all humility and honour.

So the way did not seem so long that brought us
through the straggling, dim-lighted streets of Grantsville, up to the porch of its single hostelry; where,
after some parley, I found a fair chance of supper
and bed, and a heavy-handed Orson to help me in
racking up Falcon.

It would be very unfair to draw a comparison between an ordinary road-side inn in England, and its synonym up in the country of America; a better parallel is, a speculative railway tavern verging always on bankruptcy. There is an utter absence of the old-fashioned coziness, which enables you easily to dispense with luxuries. You enter at once into a stifling stove-heated bar-room, defiled with all nicotine abominations, where, for the first few minutes, you draw your breath hard, and then settle down into a dull, uneasy stupor, conscious of nothing except a weight tightening round your temples like a band of molten iron. That is the only guest-chamber, save a parlour in the rear, the ordinary withdrawing-room and nursery of the family, where you take your meals in an atmosphere impregnated with babies and their concomitants. The fare is not so bad, after all, and monotony does not prevent chicken and ham fixings from being very acceptable after a long, fasting ride. It blew a gale that night from the N.W., and the savage wind—laden with sheets of snow—hurled itself against eaves and gable till the crazy tenement quivered from roof-tree to foundation-beams. I went to my unquiet rest early, chiefly to avoid an importunate reveller in the bar-room, who 'wished to put to the stranger a few small questions,' troublesome to answer, that I had not patience to evade.

It was high noon on the following day when I set

forth again. The snow had ceased to fall two hours
before, but I wished to give it time to settle; besides,
any tracks would greatly help me over the rough
cross-country road I had to travel. My route-bill
enjoined me to call at a certain house where the lane
turned off from the highway, to obtain further instructions. These were duly given me by the
farmer, an elderly man, with a wild, grey beard,
vague, red eyes, and a stumbling incoherence of
speech. He repeatedly professed himself 'pure and
clear as the dew of Heaven.' These characteristics
applied probably to his principles, — patriotic or
private; they certainly did not to his directions,
which led me two miles astray, before I had ridden
twice that distance; no trifling error, when you had
to struggle back over steep, broken ground, through
drifts fully girth deep.

However, as evening closed in, I 'made' Accident—
the point where I ought to have found Shipley. He
was a very good guide,—when you caught him—but
such a perfect *ignis fatuus*, when once out of sight,
that I was not at all surprised at hearing he had
gone on, the night before, to a farm house—more
safe and secluded, certainly—about sixteen miles off.
My informant offered to pilot me thither so soon as
it should be thoroughly dark. This offer I accepted
at once, only hoping that Falcon would, like myself,
consider it ' all in the day's work.'

I shall never forget my halt at Accident, if only on

account of the martyrdom I endured at the hands of
some small, pale boys, children of the house wherein
I abode. I had just settled myself to smoke a medi-
tative pipe before supper, when they came in, with a
formidable air of business about all the three : they
drew up a little bench, exactly opposite to my rock-
ing-chair, fixing themselves, and me, into a deliberate
stare. Every now and then the spokes-boy of the
party—he was the oldest, evidently, but his face was
smaller and whiter, and his eyes were more like little
black beads than those of either of his brethren—
would fire off a point-blank pistol-shot of a question ;
when this was answered or evaded, they resumed
their steady, silent gaze. I was lapsing rapidly into
a helpless imbecility of fascination, when their mother
summoned me to supper : they vanished then, with
a derisive chuckle, to which they were certainly entitled, for they had utterly discomfited the stranger
within their gates.

One more long night-ride over steep, broken forest-
ground—enlivened by certain ultramarine reminiscences of my guide, who had been a land-buccaneer
in California—brought us to the farm, far in the
bosom of the hills, where I found Shipley, buried in
a deep sleep. The sole intelligence I heard that
night related to the roan : the enfeebled constitution
of that unlucky animal had given way under rough
travel and wild weather ; he was reported to be dying;
hearing which, I could scarcely deny him great good

sense, however I might lament his lack of endurance.

The sooner it's over, the sooner to sleep,

applies, of course, to horses as well as hard-worked men.

My new host was a thorough specimen of the up-land yeoman—half hunter, half farmer, and all over a cattle-dealer. Deer and bears still abound in those hills, though the latter are not so plentiful as they were a score of years back, when B——— and his father slew thirty-three in a single season: in one conflict he lost two fingers, from his hunting-knife slipping while he was locked in the death-grapple.

The next morning broke wild and stormy, but the goodman rode out on the scout, to see how the land lay round Oakland; while he was absent we talked over our plans, and looked over his cattle to find a re-mount for my guide. The roan's malady had not been exaggerated; he was indeed in a miserable plight, suffering, I thought, from acute internal inflam-mation. After dinner we had some very pretty rifle practice, at short distances, with huge clumsy weapons. I saw a boy of sixteen put five consecutive bullets into the circumference of a half-crown at seventy-five yards.

Late in the afternoon our host returned, and we came to terms for rather a neat four-year-old filly: neither her condition nor strength was equal to the work before her; but Shipley thought that, with nursing, she would carry him through; and once in Secessia, my interest in the purchase would cease.

The roan was, of course, left behind, to be killed or
cured.   His chances of life seemed then so faint
(though the hill-farmers are no mean farriers), that I
thought he was fairly valued in the deal at thirty
dollars.   It appeared that there was increase of
vigilance throughout the frontier-guard; in Oakland
itself a full company was stationed, and strong pickets
were thrown out all around; but B—— felt confident
he could pilot us through these.

We started soon after nightfall, in the midst of a
sharp sleet-storm, not daring to delay to give the
weather time to clear; for a domiciliary visit from the
Federals was by no means improbable.   The old hunter
had not boasted too much of his local knowledge.   He
led on, through winding byeways and forest paths—
sometimes striking straight across the clearings—till
the lights of Oakland glimmered in our rear, and the
cordon of pickets was threaded; nor did he leave us
till we had reached a point whence a straight track
—well known to Shipley—would bring us down on
the North Branch of the Potomac.   Thenceforward,
my guide and I rode on alone : the moon shone out,
broad and bright, in a cloudless sky, as we climbed the
wooded spurs that lie as out-works before the main
range of the Alleghanies; and the silvery transparent
shimmer of the frost-work on the feathery fir-sprays,
was one of the most remarkable effects of reflected
light that I can remember.   The snow was more
than fetlock-deep where it lay level, and the filly tired

fearfully towards morning. She could not walk near up
to Falcon's long even stride, so I had to halt perpetually, to wait for my companion ; but in the tenth weary
hour we sighted the crazy bridge that spans the North
Branch, and by 4 a.m. on Good Friday our steeds

> Might graze at ease,
> Beyond the broad Borysthenes.

Rock, and wood, and water, were all looking their
best, under a brilliant sun, when I rose, but the object
on which I gazed with most satisfaction, was the
accursed River—circumvented at last. The solitary
green things I could find actually on the bank, were
some sprigs of cypress : these I gathered with due
formula of lustration; but the *absit omen* was spoken
in vain.

Then I wrote two or three letters, inclosing in each
the cypress-token of partial success; but these never
reached their destinations : they were prudently suppressed, three days later, by the person to whose
discretion I trusted to forward them. My correspondence being cleared off, and Falcon thoroughly
groomed, I fell back upon the resources of the little
tavern for amusement, and lighted on one scrap of
light literature, the fragment of a nameless magazine.
In this there were some good, quiet verses, that I
thought worth transcribing, were it only for the
incongruity of the place in which I found them :
perhaps they are already well known; but *I* am
ignorant even of the author's name.

MAUD.

Yes, she always loved the sea,
God's half uttered mystery;
With the murmur of its myriad shells,
   And never-ceasing roar :
It was well, that when she died,
They made Maud a grave beside
The blue pulses of the tide,
    'Neath the crags of Elsinore.

One chill red leaf-falling dawn—
Many russet autumns gone—
A lone ship with folded wings
   Lay sleeping off the lea :
Silently she came by night,
Folded wings of murky white,
Weary with their lengthened flight—
    Way-worn nursling of the sea.

Eager peasants thronged the sands ;
There were tears and clasping hands ;
But one sailor, heeding none,
   Passed thro' the churchyard-gate :
Only ' Maud,' the headstone read,—
Only Maud—was't all it said ?
Why did *he* then bow his head,
    Moaning, " Late, mine own, too late ! "

And they called her cold—God knows.
Under quiet winter-snows,
The invisible hearts of flowers
   Grow up to blossoming :
And the hearts judged calm and cold,
Might, if all their tale were told,
Seem cast in a gentler mould,
    Full of love and life and spring.

We were in the saddle again an hour before sunset ;
our next point being a log-hut on the very topmost
ridge of the Alleghanies, wherein dwelt a man said

to be better acquainted than any other in the country round, with the passes leading into the Shenandoah Valley. We ascertained, beyond a doubt, that a company was stationed at Greenland Gap, close to which it was absolutely necessary we should pass; but, with a thoroughly good local guide, we might fairly count on the same luck which had brought us safe round Oakland. Night had fallen long before we came down on the South River—a mere mountain-torrent at ordinary seasons; but now, flowing along with the broad dignity of a swift, smooth river. My guide's mare wanted shoeing, and there chanced to be a rude forge close to the ford, which is the only crossing-place since the bridge was destroyed last autumn by the Confederates. It was important that the native pilot should be secured as soon as possible (he was constantly absent from home); so I rode on alone, with directions that were easy to follow.

The smith, whose house stood but three hundred yards or so off, had told me that I had to strike straight across the ford, for a gap in the dense wood cloaked by the opposite bank. It was disagreeably dark at the water's edge, for the low moon was utterly hidden behind a thicket of cypress and pine; but I did make out a narrow opening *exactly* oppo-site; for this I headed unhesitatingly. We lost footing twice; but a mass of tangled timber above broke the current—nowhere very strong—and the water shoaled quickly under the further shore; the bottom was sound, too, just there, though the bank was steep; and Falcon answered a sharp drive of the spurs with a gallant spring that landed him on—a narrow shelf of slippery clay, hedged in on three sides by brush absolutely impenetrable. There was not room to stand firm, much less to turn safely; before I had time to think what was to be done, there was a backward slide, and a flounder; in two seconds more, I had drawn myself with some difficulty from under my horse, who lay still on his side—too wise, at first, to struggle unavailingly. If long hunting experience makes a man personally rather indifferent about accidents, it also teaches him when there is danger to the animal he rides: looking at Falcon's utter helplessness and the constrained twist of his hind-legs, which I tried in vain to straighten, I began to have uncomfortable visions of ricked backs and strained sinews: I was on the wrong side of the river, too, for help; though even the rope of a Dublin Garrison 'wrecker' would have helped but little then. Thrice the good horse made a desperate attempt to stand up, and thrice sank back again with the hoarse sigh, between pant and groan—half breathless, half despairing—that every hunting man can remember, to his cost. It was impossible to clear the saddle-bags without cutting them loose; I had drawn my knife for this purpose, when a fourth struggle (in which his fore-hoofs twice nearly struck me down) set Falcon once more on his feet—trembling, and drenched with sweat, but materially uninjured. I contrived to scramble into the saddle, and we plunged into the ford again, heading up stream, till we struck the real gap, which was at least thirty yards higher up. It is ill trusting to the accuracy of a native's *carte du pays*. Another league brought me to the way-side hut where I was instructed to ask for fresh guidance.

'Right over the big pasture, to the bars at the corner—then keep the track through the wood to the improvements—and the house was close by.' Such were the directions of the good-natured mountaineer, who offered himself to accompany me: but this I would by no means allow.

Now, an up-country pasture, freshly cleared, is a most unpleasant place to cross, after night-fall: the stumps are all left standing, and felled trees lie all about—thick as boulders on a Dartmoor hill-side; then, however, a steady moon was shining, and Falcon picked his way daintily through the timber; hopping lightly, now and then, over a trunk bigger than the rest, but never losing the faint track: we got over the high bars, too, safely—hitting them hard. The wood-path led out upon a clearing, after a while: here I was fairly puzzled. There was no sign of human habitation, except a rough hut, some hundred yards to my right, that I took to be an out-lying cattle-shed, nor a glimmer of a light anywhere.

I have not yet written the name of the man I was

seeking: contrasts of time and place made it so very remarkable, that I venture to break the rule of anonyms. Mortimer Nevil. Who would have dreamt of lighting on, perhaps, the two proudest patronymics of baronial England, in a log-hut crowning the ridge of the Alleghanies?

While I wandered hither and thither in utter bewilderment, my ear caught a sound, as of one hewing timber: I rode for it, and soon found that the hovel I had passed thrice was the desired homestead. Truly, it was fitting that the possible descendant of the King-maker should reveal himself by the rattle of his axe.

It is needless to say, that I was received courteously and kindly. The mountaineer promised his services readily; albeit he spoke by no means confidently of our chances of getting through: the company of Western Virginians that had recently marched into Greenland, was said to be unusually vigilant; only the week before, a professional blockade-runner had been captured, who had made his way backwards and forwards repeatedly, and was thoroughly conversant with the ground. The attempt could not possibly be made till the following evening: till then, Nevil promised to do his best to make Falcon and me comfortable.

How well I remember my night in the log-hut. It consisted of a single room, about sixteen feet by ten: in this lived and slept the entire family—numbering the farmer, his wife, mother, and two children. When they spoke, confidently, of finding me a bed, I fell into a great tremor and perplexity : the problem seemed to me not more easy to solve than that of the ferryman, who had to carry over a fox, a goose, and a cabbage : it was physically impossible that the large-limbed Nevil and myself should be packed into the narrow non-nuptial couch ; the only practicable arrangement involved my sharing its pillow, with the two infants, or with the ancient dame ; at the bare thought of either alternative, I shivered from head to heel. At last, with infinite difficulty, I obtained permission to sleep on my horse-rug spread on the floor, with my saddle for a bolster : when this point was once settled, I spent the evening very contentedly, basking in the blaze of the huge oaken logs : if stinted in all else, the mountaineer has always large luxury of fuel. I was curious to find out if my host knew anything of his own lineage ; but he could tell me nothing further, than that his grandfather was the first colonist of the family : oddly enough, though, in his library of three or four books, was an ancient work on heraldry ; his father had been much addicted to studying this, and was said to have been learned in the science.

At about 10 p.m. Shipley knocked at the door— fearfully wet and cold : the smith had accompanied him to the ford, so that he could not go astray, but his filly hardly struggled through the deep, strong

water. Our host found quarters for him, in the
log-hut of a brother, who dwelt a short half-mile off.

I spent all the fore-part of the next day in lounging
about, watching the sluggish sap drain out of the
sugar-maples, occasionally falling back on the female
society of the place; for The Nevil had gone forth on
the scout. It was not very lively : my hostess was
kindness itself, but the worn weary look never was off
her homely face; nor did I wonder at this when I
heard that, besides their present troubles and hardships, they had lost four children in one week of the
past winter from diphtheria; it was sad to see, how
painfully the mother clung to the two that death had
left her; she could not bear them out of her sight
for an instant. A very weird-looking cummer was
the grand-dame—with a broken, piping voice—tremulous voice and hands—and jaws that, like the stage
witch-wife's, ever munched and mumbled : she seldom spoke aloud, except to groan out a startlingly
sudden ejaculation of—' Oh, Lord,' or—' Oh dear ' :
these widows'-mites, cast into the conversational
treasury, did not greatly enhance its brilliancy.

The blue sky grew murky-white before sundown,
and night fell intensely cold. The Nevil, who guided
us on foot, had much the best of it, and I often dismounted to walk by his side. If He who sang the
praises of the ' wild north-wester ' had been with us
then, I doubt if he would not have abated of his
enthusiasm : the bitter snow-laden blast, even where

thick cover broke its vicious sweep, was enough to make the blood stand still in the veins of the veriest Viking.   After riding about ten miles, we left the rough paths we had hitherto pursued, and struck across country.   For two hours or more we forced our way slowly and painfully through bush and brake —through marshy rills and rocky burns—demolishing snake-fences whenever we broke out on a clearing.   Shipley led his mare almost the whole way; and I, who think the saddle the safest and pleasantest conveyance over ordinarily rough ground, was compelled to dismount repeatedly.

It was about one o'clock in the morning of Sunday, the 5th of April : we were then crossing some tilled grounds, intersected by frequent narrow belts of woodland.   Our course ran parallel to the mountain-road leading from Greenland to Petersburg; the former place was then nearly three miles behind us, and our guide felt certain that we had passed the outermost pickets.   It was very important that we should get housed before break of day ; so, we were on the point of breaking into the beaten track again, and had approached it within fifty yards, when suddenly, out of the dark hollow on our left, there came a hoarse shout :

"Stop !   Who are you ?   Stop, or I'll fire."

Now I have heard a challenge or two in my time, and felt certain at once that even a Federal picket would have used a more regular formula.   The same idea struck Shipley too.

" Come on," he said, " they're only citizens."

So on we went, disregarding a second and third summons in the same words. We both looked round for The Nevil; but keener eyes would have sought for him in vain; at the first sound of voices he had plunged into the dark woods above us, where a footman, knowing the country, might defy any pursuit. Peace and joy go with him ! By remaining he would only have ruined himself, without profiting us one jot.

Then three revolver shots were fired in rapid succession. To my question if he was hit, my guide answered cheerily in the negative ; neither of us guessed that one bullet had struck his mare high up in the neck; though the wound proved mortal the next day, it was scarcely perceptible, and bled altogether internally. One of those belts of woodland crossed our track about 200 yards ahead ; we crashed into this over a gap in the snake-fence; but the barrier on the further side was high and intact. Shipley had dismounted and had nearly made a breach by pulling down the rails, when the irregular challenge was repeated directly in our front, and we made out a group of three dark figures about thirty-five yards off.

" Give your names, and where you are going, or I'll fire."

" He's very fond of firing," I said in an under-tone to Shipley, and then spoke out aloud. (I saw at once the utter impossibility of escape, even if we could

L

have found our way back, without quitting our horses, which I never dreamt of.)

"If you'll come here, I'll tell you all about it."

I could not have advanced if I had wished it; in broad day the fence would have been barely practicable. I spoke those exact words in a tone purposely measured and calm, so that they should not be mistaken by our assailants: I have good reason to remember them, for they were the last I ever uttered on American ground as a free agent. They had hardly passed my lips, when a rifle cracked; I felt a dull numbing blow inside my left knee, and a sensation as if hot sealing-wax was trickling there; at the same instant, Falcon dropped under me— without a start or struggle, or sound besides a horrible choking sob—shot right through the jugular vein.

CHAPTER VIII.

THE ROAD TO AVERNUS.

BEFORE I had struggled clear of my horse, Shipley's hand was on my shoulder, and his hurried whisper in my ear.

" What shall we do ?   Will you surrender ? "

Now, though I knew already that I had escaped with a flesh-wound from a spent bullet, I felt that I could not hope to make quick tracks that night. Certain reasons—wholly independent of personal convenience—made me loth to part with my saddle-bags ; besides this, I own I shrank from the useless ignominy of being hunted down like a wild beast on the mountains.   So I answered rather impatiently—

" What the deuce would you have one do—with a dead horse and a lamed leg ?   Shift for yourself as well as you can."

Without another word I walked towards the party in our front, with an impulse I cannot now define ; it could scarcely have been seriously aggressive, for a hunting-knife was my solitary weapon ; but for one moment I *was* idiot enough to regret my lost revolver. I was travelling as a neutral and civilian, with no

other object than my private ends ; the slaughter of
an American citizen, on his own ground, would have
been simply murder, both by moral and martial law,
and I heard afterwards that our Legation could not
have interfered to prevent condign punishment. But
reason is dumb sometimes, when the instincts of the
' old Adam ' are speaking. I suppose I am not
more truculent than my fellows ; but since then, in
all calmness and sincerity, I have thanked God for
sparing me one strong temptation.

Before I had advanced ten paces the same voice
challenged again.

" Stop where you are—if you come a step nearer,
I'll shoot."

I was in no mood to listen to argument, much less
to an absurd threat.

" You may shoot and be d—d," I said. " You've
got the shooting all your own way to-night. I carry
no fire-arms"—and walked on.

Now, I record these words,—conscious that they
were thoroughly discreditable to the speaker,—simply
because I mentioned them in my examination before
the Judge Advocate, (after he had insisted on the
point of verbal accuracy), and from his office emanated
a paragraph, copied into all the Washington journals,
stating that I had cursed my captors fluently. I
affirm, on my honour, that this was the solitary
imprecation, that escaped me from first to last.

So I kept on advancing : they did *not* fire, and I

don't suppose they would have done so, even if they had had time to re-load. I soon got near enough to discern that among the three men there was not a trace of uniform; they were evidently farmers, and roughly dressed ' at that.' So I opened parley in no gentle terms, requiring their authority for what they had done, and promising that they should answer it, if there was such a thing as law in these parts.

" Well, if we ain't soldiers," the chief speaker said, " we're Home Guards, and that's the same thing here; we've as much authority as we want to back us out. Why didn't you stop, and tell us who you are, and where you're going ? "

By this time I was cool enough to reflect, and act with a purpose. For my own, as well as for his sake, I was most anxious that Shipley should escape. I knew they would not find a scrap of compromising paper on me; but he was a perfect post-carrier of dangerous documents, and a marked man besides— altogether a suspicious companion for an innocent traveller. So I began to discuss several points with my captors in a much calmer tone—demonstrat- ing that from the irregularity of their challenge we could not suppose it came from any regular picket— that there were many horse-thieves and marauders about, so that it behoved travellers to be cautious— that it would have been impossible to have explained our names, object, and destination in a breath, even if they had given more time for such reply : finally, making a virtue of necessity, I consented to accompany them to the regular out-post of Greenland, stipulating that I should have a horse to carry me and my saddle-bags ; for my knee was still bleeding, and stiffening fast.

All this debate took ten minutes at least, during which time my captors seemed to have forgotten my companion's existence, though they must have seen his figure cross the open ground when they first fired. Long before we got back to the horses, Shipley had 'vamoosed' into the mountain, carrying his light luggage with him ; only some blank envelopes were lying about, evidently dropped in the hurry of removal.

I knelt down by Falcon's side, and lifted his head out of the dark red pool in which it lay. Even in the dim light I could see the broad bright eye glazing : the death-pang came very soon ; he was too weak to struggle ; but a quick convulsive shiver ran through all the lower limbs, and, with a sickening hoarse gurgle in the throat, the last breath was drawn.

My good, stout, patient horse ! Few and evil were the days of his pilgrimage with me ; but we had begun to know and like each other well. I cannot remember to have borne a heavier heart, than when I turned away from his corpse, half shrouded already in a winding-sheet of drifting snow-flakes—seeing nothing certain in my own future, save frustrated projects and exhausted resources.

I threw my saddle-bags across Shipley's saddle, and rode slowly down, three miles, into Greenland. The filly's head drooped wearily, as she faltered on through the half-frozen mud and water; but no one guessed, till daylight broke, that she had then got her death-wound.

When we reached the hovel that was the head-quarters of the detachment, only two or three soldiers were lounging round the fire: but the news of a capture roused most of the sleepers, and the low, dim room was soon filled, suffocatingly, with a squalid crowd, in and out of uniform: prominent, in the midst, stood the long, lank, half-dressed figure of the lieutenant in command. Neither he nor his men were absolutely uncourteous, when they once recognised that I was not a Confederate spy, or a professional blockade-runner; but they were exultant, of course, and disposed to indulge in a rough jocularity, during the necessary inspection of my person and baggage.

The surgeon was a coarse edition of Maurice Quill: when he had examined my knee, and dressed it—not unskilfully—(the conical point of 'the Sharp's' bullet had just reached the bone), he took great interest in the search of my saddle-bags; desiring to be informed of the precise cost of each article. When I declined to satisfy him, he became exceedingly witty—not to say sarcastic.

"Here's a mighty curious sort of a traveller,

boys ; as don't know what nothing costs that belongs
to him, nor how he come by it," &c.

Now I was getting tired, and bored with the
whole business, and stifled with the close atmosphere
—laden with every graveolent horror ; besides, I
had not escaped from London ' chaff ' and Parisian
persiflage, to be mocked by a wild Virginian. So
I said, quite gravely :

" It's very simple ; but I don't wonder it puzzles
you. You have to pay, when you buy, out here, I dare
say. *I* haven't paid for anything for twenty years.
But, if I had known I was going to meet *you*, before
I came away I would have—looked at the bills."

Perhaps my face did not look like jesting ; anyhow, he took every word for earnest, and remained
silent for some time ; ruminating, I suppose, on the
grand simplicity of such a system of commerce.

This occupied their attention for a considerable
time ; when a party *did* start in pursuit of my companion, under the guidance of Dolley—the man who
had fired the last fatal shot—I reflected, with some
satisfaction, that the fugitive had a long two hours'
' law.' The guard-room cleared gradually; and, before
daybreak, I got some brief, broken rest—supine on
the narrowest of benches, with my crossed arms for
a pillow.

In spite of wound, and weariness, and discomfiture, I have spent a drearier time than the morning of that same Sunday. After the first awkward

feeling had passed off, my captors showed themselves
civil, and almost friendly, after their fashion. They
were very like big school-boys—those honest Volunteers—prone to rough jokes and rude horse-play
among themselves, which the commanding officer
not only sanctioned, but personally mingled with :
good-fellowship reigned supreme, to the utter sub-
version of dignity and discipline.

There were some lithe, active figures among them,
well fitted for the long forced marches for which both
Northern and Southern infantry is renowned; and
two or three rawboned giants topping six feet by
some inches; but not one powerful or athletic frame :
in many trials of strength, in wrist and arm, I did
not come across one formidable muscle.

About three o'clock—the weather had become
bright and almost warm before noon—I was lounging
about on the bank of the trout-stream that ran past
the door, with my guard at my shoulder, when I
saw a group of several figures approaching. When
they came nearer, one man lifted his cap on his
bayonet's point, and the others shouted. I could
not catch the words; but I guessed the truth:
they had run down Shipley, after all. He was so
utterly exhausted, both in mind and body, when
first brought in, that he could hardly speak : he was
not of a hardy constitution, and he had undergone
fatigue enough—to say nothing of the fearful weather
—to have broken down a more practised pedestrian.

Dolley's party were not the actual captors, though they were hard on the fugitive's trail; another squad, sent to search for some Confederates supposed to be hidden in the neighbourhood, had come upon some tracks in the snow leading to a farm-house, and there discovered my unhappy guide, sleeping the sleep of exhaustion. This was twelve miles from the spot where we parted, and he had struggled on till strength would carry him no further.

The lieutenant's face grew longer than Nature had left it, as he perused, one after another, the documents found on Shipley. Though his demeanour towards myself remained quite amicable, it was clear that he judged me, to a certain extent, by my associations; and his simple joviality was somewhat clouded by an uneasy sense of responsibility. Nevertheless, the evening passed quickly enough round the guard-room fire; the men sang some simple chants, and the deep, rough voices sounded not unmusically. Once more, I preferred a single plank to the nameless abominations of the bunks, above and below stairs; and, consequently, awoke with aching bones, but flesh intact.

The next morning we bade farewell to the Greenland detachment, in no unkindness. I was really sorry when I read in the papers, a month later, of their capture by Imboden's division, after an obstinate defence in the church, which was burned over their heads before the survivors would surrender.

New Creek, the head-quarters of Colonel Mulligan's brigade, was our destination. We had a sufficient escort, and besides, the valiant Dolley accompanied us, in the character of chief witness, as well as chief captor. His 'get up' was very remarkable, consisting of a pair of brown overalls, an old blue, uniform coat, about three sizes too small for him, and the very tallest black hat, that, as I think, I ever beheld. Slight as my wound was, it had quite crippled me for the time; a farmer, however, for a moderate consideration, found me a pony that saved my legs, at much peril to its own; for it stumbled miraculously often. Shipley began by walking, but was glad to avail himself of a chance animal half way. Dolley and two of his friends were mounted; the soldiers kept pace with us gallantly on foot.

When we started, I bore no sort of malice to that same Dolley; but, before we had got through the twenty-three miles that brought us to New Creek, I hated him intensely, as one hates the man—friend or foe—that bores you to death's door. That he should be puffed up with vain-glory, was neither unlikely nor unreasonable. His own shots were the only ones he had ever seen fired in anger. It was natural, too, that he should overestimate the importance of his capture; he had suffered from the war, in purse if not in person, and had lost two sons in the Northern army from disease, one of whom had been imprisoned for six months by the Confederates. After his first excitement had passed away, he bore himself not unkindly towards me; though, at Greenland, he did greatly bewail the darkness that had caused him to take a costly life instead of a worthless one: Falcon would have fetched five hundred dollars in those parts; even at my own valuation, *I* could not have been appraised so highly. So I listened to him twice or thrice with great patience, while he told how well he had deserved of his country; but, when he persisted in repeating the same tale, not only to me, but to every creature he encountered, the iteration became simply ' damnable.' He spoke of his dead sons in the same pompous tones of self-exaltation, with which he reckoned all other items standing to the credit side of his patriotism. Fortunately for my equanimity, I was not present when he told his own tale at New Creek; it must have been a grand Romance of History.

Yet my poor Dolley made a bad night's work of it after all. His three days' fame in local papers cost him dear. Immediately on getting out of prison, I heard —not without a savage satisfaction—that Imboden's horsemen had harried his homestead thoroughly in their last raid; Dolley only saving his life by 'running like a hare.' The Southerners know everything that goes on near their lines, and are wonderfully regular in settling scores with any registered debtor.

At New Creek I was confronted with Colonel Mulligan. His attire was anything but military;

black overalls crammed into high butcher boots, and a Garibaldi shirt of the brightest emerald green ; but his bearing was unmistakeably that of a soldier and gentleman. He treated me with the utmost courtesy. I also met with no small kindness from the adjutant of the artillery corps, an old Crimean. Unluckily, Colonel Mulligan could not deal with my case, so after a brief examination, and liberal refreshment, Shipley and myself were forwarded by rail to Wheeling, two hundred miles further west, where the district Provost Marshal was stationed.

We reached Wheeling in the early morning, and there were indulged with a most welcome bath and breakfast. Soon afterwards we stood in the presence of the Provost Marshal, Major Darr.

The figure of this functionary certainly resembles, in its square obesity, that of the great Emperor in his latter days. Possibly for this reason, Major Darr affects a Napoleonic curtness and decision of speech. Nevertheless, he was amenable to reason, and on my agreeing to pay the expenses of an escort, consented to forward me to Baltimore, to be identified. Shipley was committed at once to the military prison.

It was a long, weary journey of twenty-three hours, and I was so harassed by want of sleep, that I scarcely appreciated some really fine scenery on the Laurel and Chestnut ranges. We reached Baltimore about 3 A.M., and I despatched two notes immediately, one to the British Consul, another to my most intimate acquaintance in the city.

Both came down without delay, proffering all possible assistance. I had a regular *levee* before my guards conveyed me to the office of the Chief of Schenk's staff, to whose mercies I was consigned. Colonel Cheesebrough was civil enough ; but, in his turn, professed himself unable to deal with my case, and referred it to the General. Cæsar was not less dilatory than Felix. I never saw the potentate before whose nod Baltimore trembles, (he was unwell, I believe, or unusually sulky), but I underwent a lengthened interrogatory at the mouth of a very young and girlish-looking aide-de-camp. In the midst of this, rather an absurd incident occurred. General Schenk's head-quarters are at the Entan House. The fair daughter of a house at which I had been very intimate was to be married, that same day, and at that same house the bridegroom's party were staying. Suddenly, through an opening door, two or three of these my friends debouched upon the scene. They had not heard one word of my misadventures, so they were naturally rather surprised at finding me there, in such company. I really think that the sympathy lavished upon me in that brief interview was not so refreshing as the palpable discomfort of the unhappy *aide*, under a galling glance-fire maintained by Southern eyes, not careful to dissemble their hatred and scorn.

I was so perfectly used to being *ballotté* by this time, that it did not in anywise surprise me, to hear that I was to be sent down to Washington, to be examined by the Judge Advocate General. There was so much delay in making out commitment papers, that we lost the afternoon train. No other started before 8 P.M., so that, by the time we reached Washington, all offices would have been closed, and we must have spent the night in the Central Guard-house. I had heard enough of the foul abominations of that refuge for the imprisoned destitute, to make me determined never to cross the threshold unless under actual coercion. I said as much to the cavalry sergeant who had me in charge; suggesting that, by taking the 4 A.M. train on the following morning, we should arrive hours before the Provost Marshal's or Judge Advocate's offices were open. He was civilly rational about the whole question, and, on my parole not to attempt escape, readily consented to accompany me to a house, where I was more at home than anywhere else in Baltimore. There I remained till long after midnight : though none of us were in the best of spirits or tempers, that brief return to social life was an indescribable rest and restorative. I mention this unimportant incident chiefly because one of the charges brought against me afterwards was founded on ' my having bribed my escort, and spent the whole night at the house of a notorious Secessionist.' The poor sergeant was reduced to the ranks for dereliction of duty ; and I the more regret this, because his good nature was *not* mercenary.

We reached Washington about 6 A.M.   No offices were open before nine.   I employed the interval, partly in breakfasting with what appetite I might, partly in a visit to Percy Anderson, whose slumbers I was compelled to break by the most disagreeable of all morning apparitions—a friend in trouble.   I could only just stay long enough to receive condolences, and promises of all possible assistance—private or diplomatic ; then I betook myself to the Provost-Marshal's office, which I did not enter; thence to that of the Judge Advocate General.

I look back upon that interview with feelings of unmitigated self-contempt.   I confess to have been utterly deluded by that sleek official's sham *bon-hommie;* so that when he prayed me to be frank and explicit—' Anything that you say, I shall receive with perfect confidence,' &c., &c.—I did strive, to the best of my powers, to forget no important incident or word relative to my conduct since I landed in America; only making reservations where confession might implicate others.   An artless boy might easily have been gulled by the portly presence, the unctuous voice, and eyes that twinkled merrily through gold-rimmed glasses ; but no man of mature age can remember such a gross mistake without a hot flush of shame.

I have little cause to love the Federal Government; but I bear no grudge against any individual Unionist, with the solitary exception of the Judge-Advocate, simply because to him alone can I trace deliberately unfair dealing and intentional discourtesy. While I was in prison I sent him two letters, at long intervals; though I again committed a gross error, in addressing him as one gentleman would write to another, I cannot think this wholly excuses his coolly ignoring both communications. On the 21st of May, Major Turner's duty brought him to Carroll Place, and he remained there two full hours: the superintendent, who had conferred with the prison-surgeon on the state of my health, pressed him strongly to see me. The Judge-Advocate refused, on the ground that the case was already decided, and would be settled in a day or so, at furthest: that same afternoon he departed on a fortnight's leave, knowing right well that no step could be taken in the matter till his return. Officials are justified, I suppose, in avoiding all waste of time or trouble: perhaps it *was* more simple to *lie* to a subordinate than to risk the short discussion that an interview would have involved. I cannot guess at the especial reason which caused me to be honoured by Major Turner's enmity; certain it is, that he was *not* neutral or indifferent with regard to my case, but exerted himself very successfully to thwart any measures tending to its decision or adjustment.

During the latter days of my imprisonment, I

M

indulged more than once in a day-dream, not the less pleasant because it is wildly improbable. Should the changes and chances of this mortal life ever bring me face to face with that jovial Judge on any neutral ground, by my faith and honour I will say in his ear five short words not hard to understand. On the steps of Carroll Place, when the door opened to set me free, I sent Major Turner a message much to this effect. I devoutly hope it was delivered with the ' verbal accuracy ' of which he is so remarkably fond.

At the conclusion of the long examination the Judge-Advocate left me for a short time to obtain instructions — possibly a warrant—from Secretary Stanton ; on his return he told me that nothing could be decided till Shipley's case had been inquired into ; he assured me that the latter should be telegraphed for at once from Wheeling ; and so, with the pleasantest of smiles, and a jest on his lips, handed me over to Colonel Baker, who was already in waiting. This official's overt functions are those of a District Provost-Marshal—in reality he is the Chief of the Secret Police. There are legions of stories abroad, imputing to him the grossest oppression and venality; even strong Unionists shake their heads disparagingly, at the mention of his name.

But of Colonel Baker, from my own knowledge, I can say nothing : I simply passed through his office to the Old Capitol ; nor do I know that he in anywise influenced my after fortunes.

It appeared that my quarters were to be, not in the main building of the prison, but in a sort of *dependánce*, a couple of hundred yards off, called Carroll Place; thither I was at once removed, after a brief consultation with the officer on guard.

Mr. Wood, the Head Superintendent, soon came to welcome the new arrival, and in his first sentence gave me a specimen of the *brusquerie* of address for which he has acquired a certain notoriety.

"Mr. ——," he said; "I'm always glad to see your countrymen *here*. My father was an Englishman; but I've no sympathy with England. I was born and bred a plebeian, sir."

As I felt no particular interest in Mr. Wood's proclivities or proletarianism, I simply shrugged my shoulders, and turned away without a reply. But when, on his first visit to my room, two days' later, he repeated exactly the same formula, without variation of a syllable, I thought it better to assure him that the iteration was absolutely unnecessary, inasmuch as I had believed him on *both* points easily from the first. He was not at all disconcerted or offended, only we heard him mutter to his subordinate, when they got outside our door :—

"That's a pretty d—d high-handed sort of a chap, anyhow."

After half-an-hour's waiting I was conducted to a room on the third story, No. 20, and in a few minutes experienced that great rarity of a 'fresh sensation,'

finding myself—for the very first time in my life—
fairly under lock and key.

I had been so 'harried' of late, that I felt a
certain relief in being settled *somewhere.* The rest
of the afternoon and evening was spent in making
acquaintance with the Baltimorean blockade-runner,
my room-mate, and in exchanging dreary prison
civilities with the cells on either side, through little
tunnels pierced in the wall by former prisoners,
which allowed passage to anything of a calibre not
exceeding that of a rolled newspaper. A deep, narrow
trough, ingeniously excavated in a pine-splinter,
enabled us to pledge each other in mutual libations.
devoted to our better luck and speedy release. The
neighbours with whom I chiefly held commune, were
an Episcopalian clergyman and a captain in the
Confederate army. Of these, more hereafter. I
breathed freely when the temporary absence of my
room-mate, for exercise, left me alone—for the
first time since my capture—with my saddle-bags.
They had been in Northern custody for four days,
and subjected to the severest scrutiny : nevertheless,
they still held certain documents, that I was right
glad to see vanish in the red-heat of a fierce
log-fire.

CHAPTER IX.

CAGED BIRDS.

THE miserable first-waking—gloomiest of all hours that follow a great loss or disaster—came late to me. I had gone through a certain amount of knocking-about—mental and bodily—in the last week; and, for seven nights, the nearest approach to a bed had been the extempore couch of a railway-car. So, on an unhappy emaciated palliasse, covered by a dusty horse-rug (it took me four days to weary the jailor into concession of sheets), I slept, all noises notwith-standing, far into my first prison-day. It was pro-vokingly brilliant and warm; indeed I must, in justice to the Weather Office, allow, that its benignancy has scarcely been interrupted, since I ceased to care whether skies were foul or fair. My recollections of that first day are rather vague; but my impression is, that I had a good deal to think about, and did not in the least know how to begin. I paced up and down, as long as my knee would allow; it was still stiff and painful, though healing fast. In a room twelve feet by eight, you square the circle much too often for pleasure; but it was a week before I had any other exercise. Then, I believe, I made some attempts to improve the acquaintance of my room-mate.

He was not sullen, but, at first, somewhat saturnine and silent. The fact was that, for many days, he had been fasting from the luxuries dearest to every American heart—whisky and tobacco; for all money and clothes had been taken from him at the Provost Marshal's office, and never were returned : in these respects, after my arrival, he fared sumptuously by comparison, and abated greatly of his discontent. I might have been much more unfortunate in my companion. He was not conversational certainly, nor very amusing in any way; but he was cunning in all the small crafts of captivity, and kept our chamber swept and garnished to the best of his power. The way in which dust accumulated and renewed itself within those narrow limits, was little short of miraculous; you might brush till you were weary, and ten minutes afterwards things would look as though brooms had never been. Twining ropes out of seasand, or any other of the tasks with which wizards have baffled fiends, were not more helpless than that on which my comrade busied himself each morning. The wood-fire could not account for it; the nuisance increased when it became too warm to light anything but candles; so it must remain, another of the physical puzzles concerning which we are perpetually wondering, ' where it all comes from,' and are never likely to be satisfied.

Mr. C—— seemed by no means sanguine as to his own prospects, and took an early opportunity of advising me not to buoy myself up with hopes of speedy release. I can say, truly, that from the very first I did not so delude myself. Some of my Baltimore friends would fain have persuaded me that, in the utter absence of criminating evidence, I should not be detained long; I forbore to argue, but my opinion remained always the same. I had heard, how tenacious was the grasp of Federal officials, unless loosened by more golden oil than I could then command. I had heard, too, how slowly aid or intercession from the free outer world could penetrate these mock-bastilles, and how reluctantly the authorities would grant the supreme favour of a hearing, or trial, to any whose condemnation was not sure. So I was prepared to resign myself to anything short of a month's incarceration; but even thus, I under-estimated the hospitable urgency of my amiable entertainers.

The return-wing of the main building in which we were confined, is occupied exclusively by prisoners committed under a Secretary's warrant. These are much more closely guarded than the other inmates; but they have the advantage of being divided off into pairs, or threes at most, in their rooms, and their comforts are certainly better attended to. The regulations anent food and liquors are liberal enough; you can obtain almost anything by paying about twice its cost; but the privilege of having meals sent in, is not lightly valued by those who have once done battle with the boiled leather called ration beef, contests in which passive resistance generally prevails.

The barred window of No. 20 looks out on the narrow yard wherein ordinary captives are allowed to disport themselves for three half-hours daily. It is a very motley crowd. There are no Confederate soldiers here; all these are confined in the Old Capitol; but of every other class you may see specimens.

I will try one or two sketches. It used to amuse me to guess at the profession of a captive from outward signs, and, after a little practice, one is rarely wrong.

Those three, talking together apart, and gesticulating so vehemently, with the Hebrew stamp on every line of their dark, keen faces, are blockade-runners : they bewail their captivity more loudly than their fellows ; but, be sure, they will wriggle out, soonest of all, if freedom can be purchased by hard swearing or gold. The profits of a single successful venture are simply fabulous ; the smugglers are frequently captured with dollars on their persons by tens of thousands : they will part readily with a share of the plunder to any accommodating official, sooner than lose valuable time here; and, as for the Oath, they swallow it without a pretence at reluctance.

That group, with wild beards and long unkempt hair, clad in rough garments of every shade, from 'butternut' to hodden grey, come evidently from the far uplands of Virginia. Looking at those rough-hewn faces and fierce eyes, you can easily believe that such men are not careful to dissemble their sympathies, and would not lightly forget an injury; the chastisement of this paternal Government will change sullen disaffection into savage animosity: they will all be sent South in time, and 'it's a free fight there.' I fancy, one or two of those yeomen will see the colour of Yankee blood, before they see the old homestead again.

That pale Judas face, with scanty, hircine beard, and an expression changing often from spiteful to cunning, could belong only to a Yankee paymaster or commissary, detected in his frauds before he had made up a pile high enough to defy justice; for a swindler is not *quite* safe till he is nearly a 'milliner.' (So, was my comrade wont to pronounce millionaire.) Such cases occur daily, and the unity of shabbiness here is always diversified by some trim criminals in dark blue. Putting apparel aside, these accessions do not seem greatly to improve the respectability of the life below-stairs.

There is a very tall man, who generally manages to take his exercise at a different hour from the common herd: when he does mix with them, his well-cut clothes and spotless linen make a strange contrast with the squalor round him. He seems perfectly contented with his present lot ; he is always humming snatches of song, or chanting right lustily ; he speaks loud and freely with the few to whose converse he condescends ; and there is a gay reck-lessness about his whole bearing almost too osten-tatious to be natural. Before long you notice one peculiarity. Speaking or listening—sitting or stand-ing—walking or resting—his long, white, lissome fingers are never still ; they cannot handle the com-monest object without betraying a swift, subdued dexterity. Look closer yet, and all his glib, sham-soldier talk will not deceive you. That gallant belongs to a great army, whose spoils—if not blood-less—must be won with knife and pistol, instead of rifle and sabre ; to an Order whose squires are often knighted with no gentle *accolade*—an Order, the date of whose foundation neither herald nor historian knows, but which must last while Christendom shall endure—the Unholy Order of Industry.

The professional gamblers, here, far outnumber the turfites of England, and they apply themselves to their business from early youth with far more exclu-sive pertinacity. The richest field for their talent is barren, now that the highroad of the Mississippi is closed ; but still in every city of importance, North or South, he who would ' fight the tiger,' need not

wander far without discovering his den. In Richmond, especially, the play never was so desperate and
deep. It is unnecessary to say towards which side
the sympathies and interests of the Mercurial guild
tend. The cunning Yankee was ever too prudent to
risk much of his hard-earned gold on the chance of a
card, fairly or unfairly turned : it is only the planter,
on whom wealth flows in while he sleeps, that tempts
Fortune with a daring, near which the recklessness of
the Regency seems cautious and tame.

It is not strange that the captive knight should
accept his present position so cheerfully. Here,
he enjoys every luxury that money can buy, and
whithersoever he may be consigned, he is sure to
fall on his feet ; for it matters little to those cos-
mopolites on what spot of earth their vagrant tents
are pitched. Neither is he of the stuff that is likely
indefinitely to be detained : even this jealous government need not fear to let such an enemy go free.
My comrade—not innocent or unmindful of past
losses at *faro*—contemplating the gay cavalier with
no loving glance, growls out, "They won't bother
themselves with that rubbish long."

There is another figure, quite picturesquely repulsive, which will attract you more than if it were
pleasant to look upon. A man, exceedingly old,
stout, and lame, with red, savage eyes, and a scowl
that never lightens or breaks : it would be an equine
injustice to compare his head to a horse's ; that of

many a thoroughbred measures less in superficial inches. Clearly, a storekeeper from some remote village, where he has battened on the necessities of his neighbours for years, till he has got bloated like an ancient spider in its web. He hobbles up and down, never interchanging a word with his fellows, but unceasingly mumbling his huge toothless jaws: they say he never mutters anything but curses; if so, his daily expense in blasphemy is something fearful to contemplate. I think that cleanliness is as foreign to that horrible old creature's soul as godliness: he never shows a vestige of linen, and I am certain he sleeps in that rusty coat of bluish grey, and in that squalid cravat-rope, never untwisted since it was first donned. His offence must surely have been commerce, active and profitable, with Rebeldom, for he never can have sympathised with any living thing.

One more picture, to close the list. I ought to know that figure, long and lanky, but sinewy withal, though the head, under the fur cap, is averted still.

> Mock me not, for otherwhere, than along the greenwood fair,
> Have I ridden fast with thee.

He turns now—I knew I was right—it is my cheery host of the White Grounds, who led us so gallantly through brake, and brook, and snow-drift, when the Federal dragoons followed hard on our trail: a broad light of recognition spreads over all his honest face as he waves a stealthy salute, and I straightway go through the pantomime of drinking to his health and quick deliverance.

Women of all classes are confined here; but beauty only beams on the prison-yard from the windows of its cell. At this moment of writing, I hear voices from a room immediately below me: fair, the speakers possibly may be; but—judging from the fitful scraps of conversation that rise hither—they are assuredly *very* frail.

I think one of the most exasperating circumstances of this house of bondage, is the exceeding flimsiness of its defences. Part of the enclosure of both yards consists of tall, thin boarding, full of cracks and crevices, that might be breached with no extraordinary exertion of foot or shoulder; and there is hardly any part of the stronghold out of which a man of average ingenuity, armed with a common clasp-knife—if unwatched—could not make his way in a couple of hours. But, unwatched you never are. The passages are not more than thirty feet long, and there is a sentinel in each who can hear almost every sound from within. A state prisoner never stirs beyond his room, without an armed guard at his shoulder.

I soon heard that my reverend neighbour on the right contemplated evasion; and, considering his opportunities, I rather wondered at finding him here. In every cell there is a small closet, corresponding with those on the floor above and below. In this especial one the ceiling had fallen away, or been removed by some former prisoner; nothing but plain boards intercepted a passage to the unoccupied attic-story, where dormer windows opened on to the shingle roof.   But, with all this, it took the parson a full month to make up his mind and preparations. I often communed with him through the tunnel aforesaid, and he amused me not a little sometimes.

He looked at all things through a magnifying glass of about eighteen powers.   I know that he was perfectly honest, in the delusion of considering himself one of the most important state prisoners that had ever been confined here.   He would have it, that half Maryland was in mourning for him, and ready with ransom of untold gold; but was certain, that the Government would never venture to set him free while the war should last.   Upon the Oath of allegiance being proposed to him, instead of simply declining, he defied the judge to do his worst, expressing his readiness to confront either gallows, or platoon.   The risk of either, was about equal to that of his being tortured at the stake, on the steps of the Capitol.   In spite of all this simple vanity, and flightiness of brain, you could see that the parson had good strong principles, and held to them fast; and I believe that his nervous excitability would not have deterred him from encountering real danger. He appeared thoroughly courteous, generous, and good-natured; and my companion, to whose regiment he had been chaplain, told me that nothing could exceed his considerate kindness to the soldiers.

Albeit afflicted by occasional fits of depression, the reverend, as a rule, talked very cheerily ; but,—ah me!—how sorrowfully he would sing ! There was one psalm—penitential I presume—of about twenty-two verses, an especial favourite. This was, probably, the most soul-depressing melody that has been chanted since the days of The Captivity. The mournful monotone bore you down irresistibly ; Mark Tapley would have subsided into melancholy gloom, before the slow versicles were half dragged through. But the parson was not the only musical culprit, nor the worse, by many degrees. It would be absurd to expect much cheerfulness here : a hoarse roar breaks out now and then at some coarse practical joke ; but a frank, honest laugh—never. Yet I do wish that imprisoned discontent would vent itself otherwise than in discordant, dismal howling. At this minute, a cracked voice is droning out,

A little more cider :

—it might be a Sioux chanting his death-song.

How well I remember, in what ' stately home of England ' I first listened to that pleasant ditty. I hear, now, the leader's rich, round tones, and I see quite plainly the fair faces of the youths and virgins that made up the choir. *Bastà !* it don't bear thinking about. If mine enemy were anywhere but

round the corner, I would try if his music would
stand a volley of orange-shot.

For three days or so, I could scarcely take up a
paper without seeing my own unlucky name paraded
in one, or more paragraphs. As they all varied, it was
somewhat remarkable that, in all alike, facts should
have been so absurdly distorted. They were not
content with drawing my own fancy portrait—imagine,
if you please, the caricature—but they built up a little
romance about poor Falcon's assassin, giving him
credit for much suffering for his country's sake, par-
ticularly for long imprisonment at Richmond, since
which time he had devoted himself as an Avenger. I
was gratified to observe that his name was seldom, if
ever, correctly spelt. I did think of sending a con-
tradictory note to one of the local journals, but
decided against wasting ink and paper. Besides, it
is a pity to abase oneself unnecessarily. 'I ain't
proud, 'cos it's sinful,' nor over careful with whom
I try a fall; but I confess a preference, for more
creditable antagonists than American penny-a-liners.
So, I let them—lie.

On the fourth evening of my imprisonment, there
was an unusual stir in the building soon after nightfall.
Intercourse between the different rooms is prevented
as much as possible, but the channels of covert communication are many, and not easily cut off. In ten minutes
every one was aware, that the iron-clads which were
to annihilate Charleston had recoiled, beaten and

wounded. My mate rejoiced greatly, after his saturnine fashion, and I—the fulness of listlessness being not yet—felt a brief glow of satisfaction. Others were more demonstrative. Loud came the pæan of the warlike priest through our mural speaking-trumpet; while the sturdy soldier on the left, after hearing the news, and taking a trough-full of ' old rye,' expressed himself " good for two months more of gaol." Some one at a lower window began to sing, softly at first, the National Anthem of the South; then voice after voice joined in, in spite of sentinels' warnings, till the full volume of the defiant chorus rolled out, ringingly :

> Hurrah, hurrah ! for Southern rights, hurrah !
> One cheer more for the bonnie blue flag
> That carries a Single Star.

On the whole, I think that Sunday evening passed more rapidly than any that I can chronicle here.

The newspapers, for the next few days, were rather amusing. The well-practised Republican apologists exhausted their ingenuity in endeavouring to explain away the reverse. It was an experiment —a reconnaissance on a large scale—anything you please, but a repulse. But the facts hemmed them in remorselessly; at last, in their desperation, they fell fiercely, not only on their Democratic opponents, but on each other.

The truth is, that the failure of the iron-clads was so complete, that it ought to furnish some useful hints

N

for the future. With the exception of the Keokuk, whose construction differed slightly from that of her fellows, none were sunk or fairly riddled with shot; but scarcely one went out of that sharp, brief battle efficiently offensive. The starting of bolts might easily be remedied, but it is clear that the revolving machinery of the turrets is far too delicate and vulnerable; and that these are liable to become 'jammed' by a chance shot at any moment. This objection is the more serious, when you consider how miserably these vessels seem to steer. Almost all were more or less 'sulky' as soon as they felt the strong tide-way, and the huge Ironsides lay a helpless, useless log, half-an-hour after going into action. Neither do they appear to be very formidable, offensively. No reliable evidence proves Fort Sumter to have suffered material damage; yet the attacking force spent their strength exclusively on one of its sides and angles, and there was nothing to prevent their pouring in a concentric fire, on any weakened point or possible breach.

But a stranger soon ceases to be surprised at any trick or eccentricity of the American Press. The common courtesies and proprieties of the Fourth Estate are utterly ignored in the noisy Batrachomachia: the first step in editorial training here must be to trample on self-respect, as the renegade used to trample on the Cross. Not only do the leading articles teem with coarse personal abuse of political

opponents, but a rival journalist is often freely stigmatised by name; his antecedents are viciously dis-
sected, and the backslidings of his great-grandsire
paraded triumphantly; though this is an extreme
case, for such an authenticated ancestor seldom helps
or hampers the class of which I speak. A year of
such ignoble brawling must surely be sufficient to
annihilate more moral dignity, than most of these
small Thunderers can pretend to start with.

One is prepared for anything, after seeing whole
columns of journals, boasting no small metropolitan
and provincial renown, filled by those revolting
advertisements, that the lowest of our own penny-
papers only accept under protest.

Upon one point, certainly, all agree—constant distrust and depreciation of England; and, all things
considered, I know no one spot on God's earth,
where the hackneyed old line can be quoted so com-
placently by a Britisher :

Sibilat populus, mihi plaudo.

It would be unfair, not to give the American Press
credit for great energy and ability in collecting intelligence from the different seats of war. Considering
the vast surface over which military operations ex-
tend, and the immense distances that often lie
between the scene of action and the place of publica-
tion, it is really wonderful to see how copiously the
New York journals contrive to minister to their

readers' curiosity. The ' Herald,' in particular, has one
or more correspondents wherever a single brigade is
stationed, and according to their own accounts—which
there is no reason to doubt—they frequently accompany the troops, till actually under fire. All agents
of the Press with the army of the Potomac, are now
obliged to sign their communications with their real
name. This general-order is of course intended to
check the freedom of criticism, which has of late
become rather too plain-spoken to be agreeable to the
irascible Chief. But it is difficult to gag an undaunted ' special ; ' so every morning the last
intelligence streams forth—fresh, strong, and rather
coarsely flavoured—like new whisky from a still.

The sobriety of the weekly journals contrasts
refreshingly with the licence of their diurnal brethren.
Sporting papers are nearly the same all the world
over ; but, in the rest of these placid periodicals,
there is little of violence or virulence to be found.
They are enthusiastic about the War of course, and
occasionally querulous about the Copperheads ; but
they never quarrel among themselves, and are seldom
thoroughly savage with any one, or anything. They
generally contain a chapter or two borrowed, with or
without permission, from some English story in
progress—' Eleanor's Victory ' is the favourite now—
the rest of the non-illustrated pages are filled with
the very mildest little tales that, I think, ever were
penned.

These simple romancers in nowise resemble the vitriolic melo-dramatists — scarcely caricatured by *Punch* in ' Mokeanna,'—who try to drug, in default of intoxicating, their audience ; the liquor they proffer in their pretty flimsy cups, if not exciting, is far from deleterious ; not unfrequently you catch glimpses of an under-current of honest pathos, soon smothered by garish flowers of language; and sometimes the style sparkles into mild effervescence, redeeming itself from utter vapidity ; these ephemerals, indeed, belong rather to the lemonade than the milk-and-water class ; but, throughout, there is a woeful want of *verve* and virility.

It was inexpressibly refreshing, after loitering through twenty such pages, to revert to the ' History of the Crimean War :' the curt, nervous periods were a powerful mental tonic ; and few, of his many readers, owe so practical a debt to Mr. Kinglake as the writer of these words.

CHAPTER X.

DARK DAYS.

So—heavier with each link—the chain of days
dragged on. My room-mate soon thawed into a
stolid sociability, and was quite disposed to be communicative; but his narrative riches about matched
those of the knife-grinder, and his military experience of one year only embraced one battle—that of
Manassas. His ideas of English society were very
remarkable. The works of Mr. G. W. M. Reynolds
are much favoured, it appears, by the class who believe
in Mr. George F. Train's veracity and eloquence;
from these turbid fountains mine honest friend's con-
ceptions were drawn. I took some trouble to unde-
ceive him, and partially succeeded, chiefly by insisting
upon the fact that—of all living writers—the ingenious author of the ' Mysteries of Everything' was
probably the man least qualified, by personal experience, to discourse concerning the manners and customs of the upper, or even the educated, classes.
Slowly and reluctantly, the Baltimorean abandoned
his cherished ideal of the British aristocrat—a covert
Caligula, with all modern improvements—varying the

monotony of orgies with interludes of murder and rapine; the instrument of these pleasant vices being always ready in the shape of a Frankenstein-monster, whose mission it is to tyrannise perpetually over the guilty lordling or lady whose secret he holds; doing a steady trade of two assassinations or abductions weekly; and utterly inviolable by cord, shot, or steel, up to the final blue-fire *tableau* of the dreary drama. I believe, that my mate is now prepared to admit, that a certain amount of piety and chastity is not incompatible with tenure of the highest dignities in the Anglican church—that a youth need not necessarily be a savage Sybarite, because he happens to be heir to a dukedom—that matronly virtue may, with a struggle, be retained even by a Countess—and that a man may possibly be a kindly landlord, and even an honest farmer himself (that was the crowning triumph), though born a belted Earl.

On the fourth day, I bethought myself of teaching my companion piquet (no purely transatlantic game is in the least interesting, if the stakes are nominal): he acquired it with the ready aptitude that seems natural to Americans, and I soon had to drop the odds of the deal. We played many hundred *parties* for imaginary eagles; eventually I got a run, and left off a good winner, which, as my opponent had not money enough to buy tobacco, was highly satisfactory to every one concerned.

After a week's confinement to my room, I was allowed to take half-an-hour's exercise daily in a narrow strip of yard just twenty-one paces long; it was hedged in with kitchens and all sorts of disagreeable buildings, but the additional space was not to be despised. On the first evening after this concession, I was pacing up and down moodily (only inmates of the same room are allowed to descend together, so that you gain no social advantage), when just over my head, from a window on the first story, there broke out a burst of merriment, and a half-intelligible trill of baby-language; then a little round pink face, under a cloud of fair hair, peered out at me through the bars. The utter incongruity of the whole picture struck me so absurdly, that, I believe, I did indulge in a dreary laugh. Then the child began to talk again; and clapped its hands exultingly, as its mother caught an orange I threw up at her, when the sentinel's back was turned. So a sort of acquaintance began. Every day for a month, I saw that promising two-year-old (to whose sex I cannot speak with certainty); and I never heard it fretting or wailing. Whenever it saw me, it used to break out into a real uproarious laugh, as if our common imprisonment was the very best joke that had ever been presented to its infantile mind. I am ashamed to avow, that my own sense of the ridiculous was by no means so keen. The mother evidently pined far more than the baby; for her face grew, every day, more white and worn. What was the offence of either against the Government, I never heard; for no official or soldier will answer any question, and discourse between the prisoners is strictly forbidden. They went South, in the great exodus of the 20th of May. I contrived on that morning, with much cunning, to cast in six or seven oranges at their window, which, I hope, solaced those two Gentle Traytours through the burden and heat of the day.

Till I got too sulky and savage to seek unnecessary intercourse with any one, I found occasional amusement in 'chaffing' the sentinels. The orders against conversation with these, were not rigidly enforced. Finding that they rose very freely to the bait of a strained ironical politeness, I used to beg them to tell off by sections, the victims of their red right hands—chickens and ducks not being counted— also, I was fain to learn, how many rebel standards and pieces of cannon each man had captured and retained? If they took no credit for any such feats, I would by no means believe them, imputing the denial solely to the modesty inseparable from true courage.

Descending into the yard, one day, I found the sentry—an overgrown lad, with broad, crimson, beard-less cheeks—in a perfect paroxysm of excitement, using great freedom of gesticulation and blasphemy. I had had immense success in bewildering this par-

ticular warrior a few days previously; so I went up
to him at once:

"My blood-stained veteran," I said, "what has
roused your apoplectic valour?"

I think he was rather shamed at being caught;
but he grumbled out, sulkily rough, something about
—"If they don't keep their —— heads in, they'll
get more than they ask for." I followed the direction of his eyes, and there, on the third story, sate
two of the quietest-looking middle-aged women I
ever beheld. They were evidently new arrivals,
and had not heard of the injunction against putting
heads out of windows; for they were staring down
in blank astonishment, unconscious that the blatant
threats were levelled at them. Now, the ingenious
juggler who packed himself into a bottle, might possibly have succeeded in infringing the aforesaid rule:
no other human being could have got his cranium
through the bars. I suspect, it was simply an outbreak of the plethoric sentry's irrational ferocity (he
had been sweltering under a burning sun for two
hours) on the first helpless object that came across
him; for I could not make out that the women had
answered or aggravated him. I addressed to my
friend many compliments on his prowess—trusting
that his soldierly zeal would be appreciated in higher
quarters. Nevertheless, I presumed to suggest that
it would have been wiser to have begun with the
baby: if he could frighten that into fits, his rapid

promotion must have been ensured. I believed that Brigadier Turchin would soon want an *aide*, and who knows? &c.

In a few minutes he waxed frightfully wroth; but he had already broken the non-conversation orders, and I would not allow him to fall back upon these, now. At last, he retreated to a part of his beat where I could not follow him, and there growled and ground his teeth, till my time was up. The corporal who was my immediate guard, tried to excuse his comrade, hinting that "he wasn't quite right in the head." Possibly this may have been one of his 'off-days.' The jest of that afternoon was turned into bloody earnest, before three weeks had passed.

Not long after this, I had a pleasanter incident to chronicle. As I entered the yard one day, my guard remarked with a broad grin: "Somethin' new up there, Colonel."

The indiscriminate appropriation of military titles, here, is, of course, proverbial: though common prudence made me very careful not to claim a fictitious rank, after leaving Baltimore, where I was well known. I got a brevet-step with almost every change of place or association: disclaimers were never listened to.

Through the bars of a second-story window that fronted each turn of my tramp, I saw—this. A slight figure in the freshest summer-toilette of cool pink muslin; close braids of dark hair shading clear pale cheeks ; eyes that were made to sparkle, though the look in them then was very sad, and the languid bowing down of the small head told of something worse than weariness.

Truly, a pretty picture, though framed in such rude setting; but almost as startling, at first, as the apparition of the fair witch in the forest to Christabelle. Slightly in the background, stood a mature dame—the mother, evidently. No need to ask what their crime had been : aid and abetment of the South suggested itself, before you detected the ensign of her faith that the demoiselle still wore undauntedly—a pearl *solitaire*, fashioned as a Single Star. I may not deny, that my gloomy ' constitutional' seemed, thenceforward, a shade or two less dreary ; but, though community of suffering does much abridge ceremony, it was some days before I interchanged with the fair captives any sign beyond the mechanical lifting of my cap when I entered and left their presence, duly acknowledged from above. One evening, I chanced to be loitering almost under their window ; a low significant cough made me look up ; I saw the flash of a gold bracelet and the wave of a white hand ; and there fell at my feet, a fragrant pearly rosebud nestling in fresh green leaves. My thanks were, perforce, confined to a gesture and a dozen hurried words ; but I would the prison-beauty could believe, that fair Jane Beaufort's rose was not more prized than hers, though the first was a love-token granted to a king, the last only a graceful gift to an unlucky stranger. I suppose that most men, whose past is not utterly barren of romance, are weak enough to keep some withered flowers till they have lived memory down, and I pretend not to be wiser than my fellows. Other fragrant messengers followed in their season; but, if ever I 'win hame to mine ain countrie,' I make mine avow to enshrine that first rosebud in my *reliquaire*, with all honour and solemnity, there to abide till one of us shall be dust.

I heard from Lord Lyons about once a week. Though my letters were always answered most promptly, the replies never reached me within eight days. All correspondence, going or coming, passes the inspection of the Provost-Marshal and the Superintendent, and letters are forwarded and delivered— sooner or later—the whole thing resolving itself into a question of official memory or convenience. I did not doubt from the first, that no intercession, that could properly be exercised, would be spared. If repeated applications and strong representations could have availed, I should have been free long ago. But many autocrats might take a lesson from the insolent indifference of this Administration, when an argument or a request is to be set aside; it is exactly in proportion to the pliancy they display when confronted with demands enforced by a substantial threat. Lord Lyons' reputation for courtesy and kindness of heart stands too high to need any testimony of mine; but I cannot forbear here expressing my sense of his good offices, and I am not the less grateful, because these words are written on the fifty-sixth day of imprisonment.

To one member of the Legation, I am indebted for far more than official benevolence. On the second day after my committal, Percy Anderson brought up himself to the Old Capitol, a package containing cigars, books, newspapers, &c., which, he was told, would be transmitted to me 'right away.' I trust that the contents satisfied the critical tastes of the officer on guard; for from his clutches no fragment emerged. I never even heard of the kind intention, till weeks had passed; and, of many papers afterwards forwarded by the same hands, only one packet reached me.

All this time, my reverend neighbour was pressing on in earnest his preparations for escape. His roommate was a young Marylander, who had served some time on the staff of the Confederate army; he was captured at his own home, whither he had returned for a hurried visit, and was now detained as a 'spy:' this vague and marvellously elastic charge is always laid, when it is desirable to exclude a prisoner from the conditions of exchange. The plan of evasion was very simple. After passing through the floor into the attic, and thence out through the dormer-window, they had to crawl over about eighty

feet of shingle-roof—not slippery at all, nor particu-
larly steep—along the ridge, except where they had
to descend a little to circumvent the chimney-stacks;
this brought them to another dormer, giving admis-
sion to a house in the same block of building, but
not connected with the prison. The parson believed
this to be uninhabited; and the event proved either
that he was right, or that the inmates were friendly.
After several false starts, they decided on making the
attempt on the 1st of May.

In the twenty-four hours preceding, the reverend's
excitable nerves had been wound up to something
above concert pitch. He seemed to hold the real
risk—discovery and the bullet of a sentinel—very
cheap; but, magnifying imaginary difficulties after
his own peculiar fashion, he had come to look upon
the roof as a pass of peril, only to be accomplished
by preterhuman agility and steadiness of brain. His
fellow-adventurer, who from first to last bore himself
with a gay recklessness good to behold, laughed
all such forebodings utterly to scorn. I tried the
gentler tone of grave argument, demonstrating that
a *glissade* on shingles in dry weather was next to
impossible, and that the ridge, once gained, was
nearly as safe travelling as an ordinary mountain-
path. The parson's armour of meek obstinacy was
proof alike to reason and ridicule: he waxed not
wroth, and was thankful for any suggestion; but,
when asked to act accordingly, ever fell back on

one plaintive formula — "I am no gymnast," —
after the fashion of that exasperating child who met
all the Poet's questions and objections with the
refrain of

Master, we are seven.

These visionary terrors would have been of little
moment, if they had not induced his reverence to
persist in the use of certain machines, which were
more than likely to bring the whole adventure to grief.
These were a sort of sandals, studded with sharp
nails, that could be fitted either to hands or feet, and
no words can describe the proud satisfaction, with
which they were regarded by their simple-minded
constructor. Though I saw it was almost useless, I
tried hard to persuade him that, for any sort of climbing (where neither ice nor sharp edges were to be
feared), no engines could be so safe as bare feet and
hands; that it would be much harder to recover
himself, if a slip ensued from any strap giving way;
finally, that if the contrivance answered perfectly in
every other way, there was certain risk of what was
most to be avoided—sharp, sudden noises, likely to
strike strangely on the sentinel's ear. My friend
heard me out quite patiently, thanked me very cordially, and then—took his own way.

Everything was ready by midnight; but the start
was not made till 3 A.M., at which hour the moon
was quite down. We could talk but little, as it
was especially important not to arouse any suspicion

among the sentries; as far as I could make out,
the adventurers employed the interval very wisely, in
taking in supplies of both creature and spiritual
comforts, dividing their attention about equally between supper and devotional exercises. At last the
moment came, and they bade us farewell; the good
parson bestowing upon my unworthy self a really
pathetic benediction. If my own 'God-speed' was
less solemn, I know it was not less sincere. Then I
went to bed, and as another twenty minutes passed
without my hearing a sound, I began to think the
fugitives were well away. I was just dropping off to
sleep, when I heard voices in the yard speaking loud
and hastily, though I could not catch the words.
Then there was a scuffle of feet above, and a scrambling fall beyond the right hand wall. After a few
minutes' silence, quick steps came along the passage,
and the door of No. 22 was opened. The visitors
soon went away; but we did not know what watch
might be set, so essayed no communication with our
unlucky neighbour till the morning was far advanced.
The adventure had miscarried in this wise.

When they mounted into the empty attic they
found the window invitingly open, and, after waiting
a few minutes to humour the moon, the soldier
volunteered to reconnoitre. He reached the ridge
without the slightest difficulty, and crawled along
till he could see his way clear to the window
they wished to attain. Then he returned undis-

covered and reported progress. Now the first
mistake was making a reconnaissance at all : *vestigia
nulla retrorsum*, ought to have been the word that
night, if ever. The second and graver error was,
allowing the parson to go first, when they started in
earnest. The light lithe body of the soldier could
glide over the roof with the silent swiftness of a cat
' on the rampage ; ' the same animal, shod with
walnut-shells, suggests itself as an apt, though ir-
reverent comparison for the priestly fugitive. To
use the narrator's own words—occasionally more
forcible than elegant—

" You might have heard him two blocks off, squat-
tering and spluttering over the shingles."

Those miserable machines, when put to the proof,
made more noise than even we had imputed to them.
The prisoners over whose heads the parson passed,
heard the slipping and scratching quite plainly
though the attic floor was between them. Nevertheless he had time to reach the desired window, to
let it slip once with a resonant bang, and to slip
inside out of sight, before any alarm was raised. But
the drowsy or careless sentinel awoke to a sense of
his position, just as the second fugitive turned the
first chimney-stack ; and challenged with a threat of
shooting. The Marylander knew that the game was
up, as far as he was concerned : if he went on and
escaped the bullet, those below would have seen at
what window he entered, and the start was hopelessly

short : to persist would only have ensured two re-
captures. He certainly did the wisest thing, in retracing his way as speedily as possible. When the
guards came to No. 22, they found its solitary inmate
in bed, sleeping apparently the heavy stertorous sleep
of a deep drinker : an empty whisky-bottle gave a
colour of probability to the picture. They could get
nothing out of him then ; and, afterwards, he took the
line of having been insensibly overcome by liquor, and
so prevented from accompanying his fellow-prisoner.
The authorities could scarcely have believed the story ;
but perhaps they wished to keep the escape as quiet as
possible; at any rate the Marylander was not more
strictly guarded or severely treated than before. He
took the mishap with wonderful pluck and good
humour, and spoke rather humorously than wrath-
fully of the whole affair. Yet, as far as he knew,
he had come back to indefinite captivity. When
he went south with the rest of them on the 20th
of May, no man of the five hundred better deserved
freedom.

Some days afterwards we had news of the divine—
safe so far, and many miles away. Certainly, had he
possessed his soul in patience a fortnight or so longer,
he would have been forwarded to his desired destination securely, and at the expense of the enemy.
Before he reaches it now, he will have paid away a
sheaf of greenbacks, and run the gauntlet of a frontier
blockade, closing in more tightly every hour. North

of the Potomac there is no rest for the sole of his foot. So, many would say, that the escapade had far better have been deferred. Eight weeks ago I should have been of that same opinion, but now—I doubt— I doubt. The prospect outside ought to be very dark, and rife with peril, to induce a man to resign himself deliberately to another decameron here.*

On the 15th of May, my room-fellow was told that he was to be sent South immediately : he received the news very stolidly, and betrayed no impatience during the interval that elapsed before the exchange-steamer could be got ready. Truth to say, it is rather an equivocal advantage—to be turned loose in a city where famine-prices prevail, utterly penniless. But, if my mate did not exult in his prospects, neither did he in anyway despond. He "supposed he'd get along somehow;" indeed, he had plenty of a very useful capital—solid, persevering self-reliance.

There was great bustle in the yard on the morning of the 20th; all the men who had got the order of release, were mustered there before ten o'clock. After many delays, each person passed out singly, as his name was called, and it was high noon when the last

* Since writing the above, I have met the parson in England. I am bound to state, that he gives rather a different account of the escapade, and intimates that the Maryland youth's 'tightness' was rather real than assumed; that it was, in fact, the cause of his being left behind. It is possible that I may have been too hard on his reverence's nervousness—scarcely doing justice to his earnestness of purpose; but, as to the aforesaid infernal machines—I decline to retract one word.

prize was drawn; leaving nothing but dreary—very dreary—blanks for us whose tickets were still in the wheel. There was no uproarious merriment, or even exuberant cheerfulness in the crowd below; the satisfaction was of the saturnine sort, such as people feel who have waited long for their just dues, and have extraordinarily little to be thankful for. Once more, in dumb show, I pledged mine honest host of the White Grounds, while he responded in a stealthy *duc-an-dhurras;* then, having furnished my mate with such provant as was available, I wished him, too, sincerely good-speed.

I cannot say that I was sorry, at first, to find myself quite alone. I am ashamed to confess that I had been daily growing more sullen and unsocial: upon reflection, I think, I had decidedly begun to tyrannise over my companion; some of his harmless peculiarities which I hardly noticed at first, would, at times, irritate me savagely: besides, every cubic inch of vacant space has its value in a low-browed room twelve feet by eight, when the thermometer means mounting in earnest. But, as the dreary time dragged on, and as the leaden listlessness settled down heavier hour by hour, I began to look back regretfully, if not remorsefully. There were moments, not few or far between, when I would have given much to hear the wire-drawn monotone that lately had been an offence to me; ay, even though each slow sentence should be punctuated by expectoration.

Among those who were exempted from the gaol-delivery was an Englishman, John Hardcastle by name, who had been arrested about a month later than myself, on the Lower Potomac, on his way homeward through the Northern States. He had, I believe, been employed by the Confederate Government in carrying out some inventions and improvements in armoury. There was nothing remarkable about the little, round, ruddy man, except a joviality which never seemed to droop in the heavy prison-air; when I wrote that an honest laugh was never heard here, I ought to have made that one exception; he had a fair voice, too, and a large collection of songs, which he chanted out merrily, instead of merging all tunes into one dolorous drone. He was confined at first on the floor immediately under me; but, on the 20th of May, changed his quarters into one of the large rooms in the main building, with windows opening back and front into the yard and the Avenue: these latter were without bars. All through the evening of Sunday the 24th I listened, rather enviously, to Hardcastle's noisy mirth: his voice never ceased to rattle—now bantering a fellow-prisoner with good-natured aggravation—now shouting out a verse of some popular song — now declaiming a sentence or so of exaggerated mock-oratory; yet he did not give me the idea of being uproarious with drink (I heard afterwards he was perfectly sober); rather, he seemed possessed by an exhilaration involuntary and irrational, like a person who has inhaled laughing-gas. It was not till next day that the Highland word ' Fey ' came into my mind. I am scarcely inclined, now, wholly to deride that old superstition. Is it possible, that the foreshadow of doom does, in some mysterious way, affect certain nervous systems, when the soul, within a few hours, must pass out free through the rugged doors of violent death ?

About eleven o'clock on the following morning I heard a rifle-shot, but took little heed of it, as I knew that accidental discharges from careless handling of firelocks were not uncommon. Shortly afterwards, the officer of the keys asked me to visit the Superintendent in his room. It was natural, that such a summons should conjure up certain faint hopes of approaching liberation; or, at least, of the ' hearing' so long deferred. All such visions vanished instantly at the first sight of the official's face, as he met me in the doorway : no good tidings for any one were written there ; I knew that some grave disaster had occurred, before my eye lighted on the table, strewn with papers, letters, and banknotes—all dabbled with the dull, red blots that marked the hand of Cain.

In a very few words—spoken in a low hoarse voice, strangely changed from its wonted boisterous loudness —the Superintendent told me why I was wanted there. A British subject had just been shot by a sentinel

for transgressing the window-order mentioned above;
as 800 dollars in Confederate notes, besides other
valuables, were found on his person, it was thought
well that I should assist at the inventory and
attest its correctness. It seemed that some hasty
words of the Superintendent, reflecting on the
remissness of the soldiers on duty, had been the
proximate cause of the slaughter. I do believe, that
the death-warrant was unwittingly spoken. The
man's bearing and demeanour are rough, even to
coarseness, and his sensibilities probably blunted
from having perpetually to listen to complaints and
tales of wrong-doing, which he must perforce ignore;
but I do not think his nature is harsh or cruel; the
bark of Cerberus is much worse than the bite;
and he is quite capable of benevolent actions,
done in an uncouth way. The lips of the corpse upstairs were scarcely whiter than those, that kept
working and muttering nervously close by my
shoulder, as I sat at my ghastly task. I was right glad
when all was ended, and I had escaped from the small
close room, where the air seemed heavy with the
savour of blood. All that day, there lay upon the
prison-house a weight and a gloom, that came not
from the murky, windless sky; the few faces that
showed themselves in the yard looked more dark
and sullen than ever; and men, gathering in knots
instead of pacing to and fro, murmured or whispered
eagerly. My unlucky head chanced to be more

troublesome than usual; altogether, I cannot look back upon a more depressing evening.

About noon on the following day a tawdry coffin of polished elm, beaded and plated wherever there was room for a scrap of silvered metal, was laid on chairs in the prison-yard; and, soon, all those who had access to that part of the building gathered round it —listening, uncovered, to the scanty rites, which the Old Capitol concedes to prisoners released by that Power, in presence of whose claims the *habeas corpus* is never suspended. A tall lank-haired man, looking more like an undertaker than a divine of any denomination, read straight through, without a syllable of preface, the fifteenth chapter of the First Epistle to the Corinthians, and then, kneeling down, began a rambling extemporaneous prayer, the main object of which seemed to be, to address the Deity by as many periphrastic adjurations as possible. The orator besought, ' that these melancholy circumstances might be blessed to us the survivors;' and rehearsed several platitudes on the uncertainty of life; but, from first to last, there was not one single word of intercession or commendation on behalf of the dead man's soul. I was glad when it was over: our own simple service, read by the merest layman, would surely have been a more fitting obsequy.

What followed, was startling enough from its very suddenness. One of the assistants stepped forward and, with a quick careless motion, threw back two folding shutters that formed the upper part of the coffin-lid : the blaze of the vertical sun, on which no living thing could have looked unblinded, fell full on the heavy eyelids that never shrunk or shivered, and on the bare upturned features, blanched to the unnatural whiteness only found in corpses from which the life-blood has been drained away. Since then, I have tried to recall the face as I saw it often—round and ruddy, beaming with reckless joviality and grotesque humour : it will only rise as I saw it once—white, and solemn, and still. When the crowd had satisfied their curiosity, the coffin was borne away, and everything fell back into the old groove of monotony.

It will hardly be believed that, though the victim had communicated more than once with the British Legation (an envelope franked by Lord Lyons was among the papers I examined), the Federal authorities did not deem it necessary to give any official notice of the slaughter. Percy Anderson was absolutely ignorant of what had happened, when he came to me on the following day. The fact, too, is significant, that the Washington journals, for whose net no incident is generally too small, made no allusion to the tragedy, till the Thursday morning ; I presume silence was considered useless when a member of our Legation must have been made acquainted with the details.

The regrets of those who may have been interested in poor John Hardcastle's life and death, will scarcely be lessened by the knowledge, that he was not

even in fault when he suffered. There were eight or
ten prisoners confined in the same room ; and it was
one of his companions who had previously been twice
warned back by the sentinel: he himself was shot
almost instantaneously after his head was thrust forth,
without a second challenge. The Washington papers
stated that, when ordered to draw back, he refused
with an oath. With such chroniclers one would not
bandy contradictions ; I give this version of the facts,
as I received it from the lips of the Superintendent.

Late in the afternoon of Wednesday, the 27th, I
was again summoned below. I found Percy Anderson
waiting there: he had obtained from the War Office
an order to see me alone, without limitation of time. I
understood that there was no precedent for such a
concession ; the general rule being, that prisoners
should only receive their friends in the presence of an
officer, who is bound to watch and listen jealously,
while no interview can be extended beyond fifteen
minutes. Never surely was a call better timed. I was at
my very worst, just then ; besides a couple of potatoes
and a crust of dry bread, no solid food had passed my
lips for seventy hours. Of my personal appearance,
from my own knowledge, I can say nothing (for my
mate and I had agreed in considering mirrors superfluous luxuries); but, from the startling effect produced
on my visitor, I fancy that the dreary week of weeks
had made wild work with the outward, as well as
inward man. I know that the kind diplomatist was

more than pained, at finding himself unable to give
me any foothold of certain or substantial hope ; it was
impossible to hazard a reliable guess as to the termination of my confinement. Hitherto, the unceasing efforts
of the Legation had spent themselves on the passive
obstinacy of the Federal Government like bullets on a
cotton bale ; of a truth it was long before those Unjust
Judges grew aweary. Nevertheless, the mere sight
and sound of a frank English face and voice were
more effectual restoratives, than all the cunning tonics
and incentives, with which the prison-surgeon had
been striving to quicken an imperceptible pulse,
and to revive a deceased appetite. I have always
thought since, that the rest at that one conversational
oasis, just enabled me to hold on to the hither verge
of Sahara.

The next eight days seem nearly blank to me now.
I was past reading anything, for I could scarcely make
out the capitals with which the journalists headed their
daily bits of romance from Vicksburgh and elsewhere.
It was with great difficulty that I scrawled detached
sentences, at long intervals—a difficulty that, I fear,
some unhappy compositor, doomed to decipher the
foregoing pages, will thoroughly appreciate, though he
may decline to sympathise with.

I had one passage of arms with the Superintendent
during that week. I have an idea that I spoke
somewhat freely with regard to the Administration that he had the honour to serve, pressing him

for a justification of its conduct in my own especial case.

The official listened quite coolly and calmly, with a twinkle of amusement in his shrewd cynical eyes, and answered—

"Well, we've had a good bit of trouble with England and English this year; and I reckon they think they've got a pretty fair-sized fish now, and mean to keep him, whether or no."

"That's Republican justice, all over," I said; " to make the one that you can catch, pay for the dozen that you can't, or that you are afraid to grapple with."

"I don't know about justice," was the reply ; " but it's d—d good policy."

And so we parted—not a whit worse friends than before.

> Delicta, majorum, immeritus lues,

if memory had not failed me, I might have quoted that line often and appropriately enough. But every agent in 'the robbery,'—from the vainglorious Virginian, my chief captor, down to the smooth Secretary, whose velvet gripe was so loth to unclose,—seemed provokingly bent on exaggerating the importance of their prize. Perhaps the very interest felt in my release, and the exertions unsparingly used—especially in Baltimore—to secure it, strengthened the false impressions or pretences of the Federal powers. I write in the firm assurance that no Southern friend will deem these words ungracious or ungrateful.

There is no stone, above or below ground, white enough to mark, worthily, in my calendar, the fifth day of last June. I hereby abjure, for evermore, any superstitious prejudice against the ill luck of Fridays. Late in the afternoon I was pacing to and fro in the narrow exercise-ground, speculating idly as to the delay of my dinner, which was overdue—not that I felt any interest in the subject, but it was a sort of break and fresh starting-point in the monotony of hours—when I was summoned once more into official presence. They took me to the room on the ground-floor, where I had waited on the first day of my imprisonment while the cell above was preparing. I found there, the lieutenant commanding the guard, and two or three more officers, one of whom, I understood, was a deputy of the Judge-Advocate. They read out a paper of which the following is an exact copy, and asked if I had any objection to sign it :—

DISTRICT OF COLUMBIA, }
COUNTY OF WASHINGTON. }

Old Capitol Prison, Washington, D.C.

I, —————, of ———, in England, do solemnly swear on my Parole of Honour, that I will leave the United States of America with as little delay as possible, and that I will not return there during the existing rebellion.

So help me God.

Signed, —————.

Sworn to and subscribed before me,
    this fifth day of June, A.D. 1863.
            JOHN A. LOVELL,
                Lieut. Comdg. Guard.

Now, had I been offered a free passage South, I doubt if I should have accepted it, then; the aspect of things within the last two months had changed for me entirely. I could not hope to carry out one of my original plans; for all available resources were nearly exhausted, and procuring fresh supplies from home would have involved infinite difficulty and delay. Besides, a refusal gave at once to the Federal authorities the pretext for detention that they had sought so eagerly, and, so far, failed to find. I know no earthly consideration, excepting clear obligations of duty or honour, that would have persuaded me to incur ten more prison days. If, instead of being a free agent, I had been bound by an oath to penetrate into Secessia at all hazards, I should have held myself at that moment amply assoilzied of my vow. So, with the remark, —"that, of all the places on this earth, the Northern States of America was the country I most wished to leave and least cared to revisit,"—I signed the parole, and confirmed it with an oath.

Then, it appeared that my debt to the Union was paid, so that it had no further lien on my effects or me. The saddle-bags were soon packed; in another half-hour, I stood outside the prison-door, —realising, with a dull, dazed feeling of strangeness and novelty, that there was not the shadow of bolt, bar, or wall between me and the clear sultry skies.

CHAPTER XI.

Now that this personal narrative is drawing rapidly to its close, there is one point to which I must needs allude, at the risk of sinning egotistically. While under lock and key, I never ventured to grapple with the subject. Even now—sitting in a pleasant room, with windows opening down on a trim lawn studded with flower-jewels and girdled with the mottled belts of velvet-green that are the glory of Devonian shrub-land, beyond which Torbay shimmers broad and blue under the breezy summer weather,— I shrink from it with a strange reluctance that I cannot shake off, though it shames me.

I speak of the effect—moral, intellectual, and physical—produced by those eight weeks of imprisonment.

I do not wish to intimate that there were any actual hardships beyond the prevention of free air and exercise to be endured. More than this: I am ready and willing to allow, that certain privileges were conceded to me that I had no right to claim, which were granted to few, if any, of my fellows in misfortune. The corporal of the keys had been a clerk in the house of Ticknor and Field, the great Boston publishers, before he became a soldier; and was disposed to show every consideration and indulgence to one whom he was pleased to consider a brother of the Literate Guild. The Under-superintendent— Donnelly by name—treated me with a benevolence quite paternal. The monotony of my solitary confinement was often broken by his rambling chat and reminiscences of a gambler's life in the Far West; for he liked nothing better than lingering in my cell for an hour or so, when his day's work was done. After the prison doors were opened, I lingered for ten minutes within them, to exchange a farewell hand-grip with that quaint, kind old man. There was a stringent curfew-order enjoining the extinguishment of all lights at 9 P.M.; but on condition of veiling my window with a horse-rug, so as not to establish a bad precedent, I was allowed to keep mine burning at discretion.

Now, some readers of these pages may think that a confinement, such as I have described, wherein there was to be obtained a sufficiency, of meat, drink, tobacco, and light literature, is not, after all, a *peine forte et dure;* and that it is both weak and unreasonable thereanent to make one's moan. So— in bygone days, when the lazy fit was strong—have I thought myself. I am not malicious enough to wish, that the most contemptuously sceptical of critics

P

may be undeceived, at the price which I paid for the learning. It is possible that a person of settled sedentary habits, endowed not only with powerful resources within himself, but also with the ornament of a meek and quiet spirit, might hold out well enough for a while, more especially if supported by the reflection that he was suffering either for his country's good or for his own private advantage. But, take the converse example, of a man unsupported by any consolations of patriotism or peculation; of a temperament somewhat impatient and prone to anger, accustomed, too, from youth upwards, to constant habits of strong out-door exercise; with such an one I fancy it will fare—very much as it fared with me. Many will tell you that a few months' confinement within four walls, without stint of food or aggravation of punishment, will bring an athletic Red Indian to the extreme of bodily prostration, if not to mortal sickness. It is humiliating to confess, but I fear unhappily true that, in despite of all advantages of civilised education, some of us, under like circumstances, will go down as helplessly as the Noble Savage.

Would you like to hear of the process? It is not pleasant to look upon, or to tell.

The first few days are spent in an uneasy, irritable expectation that every hour will bring some news— good or bad—from the world without, bearing on your own especial case : then comes the frame of

mind wherein you allow that there must be certain
official delays, and begin to calculate, wearily, how
far the wire-drawn formalities will be protracted,
making a liberal margin for unexpected contingencies:
this phase soon passes away : next comes the bitter,
up-hill fight of hoping against hope ; how long this
may endure depends much on temperament—more
on bodily health ; but in most cases it is soon over,
and is succeeded by the last state, ten thousand times
worse than the first : slowly, but very surely, the dense
black cloud of utter listlessness settles down, never
broken thereafter save by brief flashes of a futile,
irrational ferocity. All your ideas move round like
tired mill-horses, in the narrowest circle, with an
unhappy Ipse Ego for its centre ; all the passing
events of the outward world seem unnaturally dwarfed
and distant, as if seen through an inverted telescope ;
the struggles of stranger nations move you no more
than the battles on an ant-hill; the only question of
civil or religious liberty in which you feel the faintest
interest is the unimportant one involving your own
personal freedom. And throughout, you are shame-
fully conscious that this indifference is not philosophical, but simply selfish.

So much for the *morale*. Does the *physique* fare
better ?

When you enter the gaol, there is probably laid up
in your lungs a certain store of fresh, free air, which
takes some time to exhaust itself ; but soon you begin

to draw your breath more and more slowly, and to
feel that the atmosphere inhaled no longer refreshes
you; no wonder—it is laden with compressed animal
life.   Then a dull hot weight closes round your brows
as if a heavy, fever-stricken hand was always clasping
them; there it lies—at night, when the drowsiness
which is *not* sleep overcomes you—in the morning,
when you wake, with damp linen and dank hair :
plunge your forehead in ice-cold water ; before the
drops have dried there it is burning—burning again.
The distaste for all food grows upon you, till it becomes a loathing not to be driven away by bitters or
quinine; there is no savour in the smoke of Kinne-
kinnick, nor any flavour left in the stilled waters
of Monongahela.   Physical prostration of necessity
speedily ensues.   Let me mention one fact—not in
vaunting, but in proof that I do not speak idly.
When we were trying those athletics at Greenland,
the day after my capture, I could rend a broad linen
band fastened tightly round my upper arm, by
bending the *biceps :* when I had been a month in
Carroll Place, I had to halt, at least once, from
absolute breathlessness and debility on the stairs
leading from the yard to the third story ; my pulse
was almost imperceptible.   By that time my sight
had become so seriously affected that I was absolutely unable to read the clearest print; even now,
a month after my enfranchisement, though keen
Atlantic breezes and home comforts have worked

wonders, I cannot write five consecutive sentences without a respite.

I am forced to quote my own experience ; but I know that it could be matched, if not exceeded, by very many cases of equal or worse suffering.

There is a very sad corollary to the foregoing statements. Captain Wynne, S.F.G., was arrested shortly before my arrival in America, on his way back to Canada after a brief tour in the South : he was confined in the main building of the Old Capitol ; from whence, after every effort to obtain his release had failed, he eventually made his escape, with equal adroitness and courage. But he carried away with him the seeds of fatal disease : I believe I am justified in asserting that his death, which occurred in London about two months ago, is attributable to the effects of imprisonment.

Long confinement presses, of course, infinitely harder on a stranger than on a native. The latter can never quite divest himself of an interest in passing events, which the former, at the best of times, can but faintly share : besides which, most Americans —not purely political prisoners—have either a definite term of captivity to look forward to, or are, in one way or other, subject to the chances of exchange.

If the Federal Government had avowed at once, that it was their sovereign pleasure to keep an Englishman in durance for a *certain* period, without attempting to excuse the arbitrary stretch of autho-

rity, one would have chafed, I suppose, under the
injustice, but still submitted, as it is the duty of
manhood to submit, to any inevitable necessity.
The doubt and indefiniteness of the whole affair,
made it inexpressibly exasperating. It was bad
enough, to have no palpable adversary to grapple
with : it was worse, to have no specific charge. As I
had contravened a General Order by crossing the
Federal lines without a pass, the Legation did not
apply for my unconditional release : it merely pressed
for the inquiry and trial that in most civilised countries a criminal can claim as a right. I was never
confronted with any judicial authority from the
moment that I entered the prison doors till they
opened to let me go free ; I never received any
official intimation of the reasons for my prolonged
detention ; and Lord Lyons' repeated applications
were at last only met by a vague assertion that they
' had reason to believe that an aide-de-camp's com-
mission, signed by General Lee, had reached me at
Baltimore.' There was not, of course, the faintest
scintilla of evidence to establish anything of the sort.
While in America I received no communication whatever—written or verbal—from any person connected
with the Confederate Government or army.

I do honestly affirm that, in dilating on the several
hardships of my own especial case, I have no idea of
enlisting any sympathy, public or private. I simply
wish to show what arbitrary oppression can be exer-

cised upon British subjects, with perfect impunity, by a Government which will maintain quasi-friendly relations with our own, just so long as it confirms the standing-ground of a tottering Cabinet. Perhaps, some day or other, as a last peace-offering to the Republican Hydra, MM. Seward and Stanton will 'burn a bishop,' and so bring our pacific Foreign Office to bay.

Physical causes prevented my feeling very exhilarated or exultant during my earliest hours of freedom. It was pleasant, though, to meet an English face at the hotel where I meant to sleep. I had not seen Mr. Austin since we were contemporaries at Oxford; but on the 2nd June I had received from him a very kind and courteous note, offering a visit, if it should be acceptable. I need scarcely say how welcome it would have been; but he did not get my written reply till the following Monday—not bad time, either, for the Old Capitol post-office. I dined with Mr. Austin, and at the same table sate General Martindale, military commander at Washington, and Senator Sumner. The former certainly recognised my identity; but he was not the less amicable for that. It was odd to find myself receiving suggestions as to my route, in case I visited Niagara, from the same man who three days before had granted a pass to my friend for his proposed prison-visit. I sate some time after dinner in talk with Mr. Sumner. His face is much aged and careworn

since I first saw it, some years ago, in England: but his manner retains the polished geniality,
which made him so great a favourite in most European *salons*.

The rest of the evening I spent at Percy Anderson's. I much regretted that I could not see Lord
Lyons, to express my sense of his unwearied exertions in my behalf; but he was dining out; and it
was judged better that I should not risk an apparent
infringement of my parole by lingering in Washington an unnecessary hour the next morning; so I
was forced to trust my thanks to writing.

I can never forget, while I live, the welcomes which
waited me in Baltimore; welcomes much too cordial
to be wasted on a discomfited adventurer. Still I was
glad to find that those, whose opinion was well worth
having, gave me credit for having deserved success.
I was very, very loth to leave my kind friends;
though we may perchance foregather again should
I outlive my parole, and be enabled to carry out
certain half-formed plans of hunting in the Far West.
It was only the sternest sense of duty that impelled
me to sacrifice to Niagara, sixty hours that intervened
before June the 13th, when the Inman steamer
started, in which I had secured a berth by telegraph.

Twenty-two hours of unbroken rail-travel—partly
through the beautiful Susquehannah Valley; partly
through the best cultivated lands (about Troy and
Elmira) that I saw in the States, where trim

stone walls reminded one of part of the Heythrop and Cotswold countries—brought us to Buffalo. The Company had here so contrived matters, that it was absolutely impossible for the traveller to proceed farther that night, or to get at any luggage beyond what he carried in his hand: from Elmira, it travels by a route of its own, to which your through-ticket does not apply: the baggage-agent hands it over to you at Niagara the next morning, with a cheerfully placid face, as if rather proud of the satisfactory correctness of the whole arrangement.

I will not add a stone to the descriptive cairn heaped up by generations of tourists in honour of the King-Cataract; simply because it is presumption in any man to pass judgment on that famous scene till he has studied it for more days than I could spare hours. I do not think the eye is disappointed, even at first sight: after being fully prepared by Church's vivid picture—a very triumph of transparent colouring—you still stand dumb in honest admiration of that one Miracle in the midst of wonders—the central curve of the Horse-shoe—where the main current plunges over the verge, without a ripple to break the grandeur of the clear, smooth chrysoprase; flashing back the sunlight through a filmy lace-work of foam. The ear is certainly dissatisfied: perhaps my acoustics were out of order, as well as other cephalic organs; but it struck me that Niagara hardly made any noise at all. Yet I penetrated under the Fall as far as there is practicable foot-hold; and listened, at all sorts of distances, for a *deafening* roar, which never came.

Eastward ho! again—by that same night's express. I cannot let this, my last experience, pass, without recording my vote on the much-mooted question of American railway travel. The natives, of course, extol the whole system as one of the greatest of their institutions; but I cannot understand any difference of opinion among strangers. The baggage arrangement—except when the Company suffers under an aberration of intellect, such as I have mentioned on the Niagara route—is really convenient, and the *commissionnaires* attached to every train relieve you of all responsibility at your journey's end, by collecting your effects, and transporting them to any given direction; but this solitary advantage does not counterbalance other *désagrémens*. When the weather is such as to allow a true current of air to circulate through the cars, the atmosphere is barely endurable : but with stoves at work, and all apertures closed, it soon becomes dangerously oppressive. The German element prevails strongly throughout Yankeeland ; perhaps this accounts for the natives' dread of fresh air. Your only chance of escaping semi-suffocation is, to secure a seat next to a window, and keep it open; hardening your heart against all the grumbling of your neighbours, who run through a whole gamut of complaints, in the

hope of softening or shaming the Hyperborean.
Sometimes you will have to encounter menaces; but,
in such a cause, it is surely worth while to do battle
to the death; revolver and bowie-knife lose their
terrors in the presence of imminent asphyxia. The
advocates of the system chiefly insist on the luxury
of the sleeping-cars, and the advantage of passing
from one end of the train to the other at your
pleasure. On the first of these points let me say,
that few aliens, after one trusting experiment of those
stifling berths, will be inclined to repeat it: the
atmosphere of a crowded steamboat cabin is pure and
fresh by comparison. As for the vaunted promenade
—the man who would avail himself thereof, would
probably waltz with grace and comfort to himself on
the deck of the Lively Sally in a sea-way: it requires
some practice even to stand upright without holding on; the jolting and oscillation are such, that,
I think, you take rather more involuntary exercise
than on the back of a cantering cover-hack. The
pace is not such as to make much amends: from
twenty to twenty-five miles an hour is the outside
speed even of expresses; and on many lines you
ought to calculate the probabilities of arrival by
anything rather than the time-tables. Collisions,
however, are certainly rare: the most common accident is when a train breaks through one of the
crazy wooden bridges, or, obeying the direction of
some playfully eccentric pointsman, plunges head-

long over an embankment into the peaceful valley
below. The steam-signals are very peculiar : the
engine never whistles, but indulges in a prolonged
bellow, very like the hideous sounds emitted by that
hideous semi-brute, yclept the Gong-Donkey, who
used to haunt our race-courses some years ago—
making weak-minded men start, and strong-minded
women scream with his unearthly roaring. When I
first heard the hoarse warning-note boom through the
night, a shudder of reminiscence came over me; for
I used to shrink from that awful Creature with a
repugnance such as I never felt for any other living
thing.

All the weariness of the long night-journey will not
prevent a traveller from appreciating the superb
Hudson, along whose banks the last part of the road,
from Albany, is carried. You are seldom out of sight
of the Katskill Range—blue in the distance or dark
in the foreground—but the crowning glory of the
river are the Cliffs, where the rock soars up sheer
from the water's edge, with no more vegetation on
its face than will grow in the crevices of ancient walls.

I had scarcely twenty-four hours left for the Im-
perial City before the Edinburgh sailed. This time, I
abode at the New York Hotel, where a Baltimorean
had already secured my quarters. Thus much, at least,
must be conceded to the Yankee capital. In no other
town that I know of can a traveller so thoroughly
take his ease in his inn. These magnificent *caravan-*

serais cast far into the shade the best managed establishments of London, Paris, or Vienna, simply
because luxuries, sufficient to satiate any moderate
desires, are furnished at fixed prices that need not
alarm the most economical traveller. The *cuisine* at
the New York Hotel is really artistic, and the attend-
ance quite perfect. Also is found there a certain
Château Margaux of '48 : after savouring that rich
liquid velvet, you will not wonder that the house has
long been a favourite with the Southern Sybarites.
Things are changed, of course, and many of
Mr. Cranstoun's old patrons now exercise their
critical tastes on mountain whisky and ration beef ;
but the tone of feeling in the establishment remains
the same. An out-spoken Republican or Abolitionist
would not meet a cordial welcome from the present
frequenters of the New York, nor, I think, from its
jovial host.

Likewise the Empress City can boast, that
her barbers and iced drinks do actually ' beat all
creation.' After a long journey, you are thoroughly
disposed to appreciate these scientific tonsors, whose
delicacy of manipulation is unequalled in Europe.
Only the pen of that eloquent writer, who told the
' Times' how he 'thirsted in the desert,' could do
justice to the high-art triumphs of the cunning bar-
keeper.

' Joe,'—of the mirthful eye, and agile hand, and
ready repartee,—long may you flourish, mitigating

the fierce summer thirst of many a parched palate ;
stimulating withered appetites till they hunger anew
for the flesh-pots; warming the heart-cockles of
departing voyagers till they laugh the keen breezes of
the Bay to scorn. With me, at least, gratitude for
repeated refreshment shall long keep your memory
green—green as the mint-sprays that, when your last
' julep ' is mingled, should surely be strewn unsparingly on your grave.

I never felt quite clear of Federaldom, till I set my
foot firm on the deck of the good ship Edinburgh. I
did not indulge in a soliloquy even then ; so I certainly
shall not inflict on *you* any rhapsodies about Freedom ;
but, in good truth, the sensation was too agreeable to
be easily forgotten.

The homeward voyage was as great a ' success,' as
unbroken fine weather, favourable winds, and company
both pleasant and fair, could make it. On the thir-
teenth day, towards evening, I found myself in the
familiar Adelphi, at Liverpool, savouring some clear
turtle ; not with a less relish because, in the accurately
pale face of the waiter who brought in the lordly
dish, there was not the faintest yellow tinge, nor a
ripple of ' wool ' in his hair.

All of my personal narrative that could possibly
interest the most indulgent public is told now ; if the
few words I have left to say should bore you—O,
patient   reader ! — they   will   at   least   be   free   of
egotism.

CHAPTER XII.

A POPULAR ARMAMENT.

It was ordained, that the Navy should reap all the bays and the rue that were to be gathered in the warfare of this spring. The amphibious failures in the south-west involved no graver consequences, than a vast futile expenditure of Northern time, money, and men; such waste has been too common, of late, to excite much popular disgust or surprise. In other parts, the keenest correspondent has been put to great straits for memorable matter; for a skirmish or a raid, even on a large scale, can hardly carry much beyond a local interest.

On the last day of April, the summer land-campaign began in earnest, when its truculent commander led the 'finest army on the planet' across the Rappahannock, unopposed.

If all other warlike music was prudently silent then, be sure, the general's own private trumpet flourished very sonorously; indeed, for many days past, it had not ceased to ring. Few armaments have set forth under more pompous auspices. First came the great review, graced by the presence of the White

House Court, who witnessed the marching past of the biennial veterans with perfect patience, if not satisfaction. The 'specials' of the Republican papers outdid themselves on that occasion; magnificently ignoring his temporary dignity, they hesitated not to compare each member of the President's family with a corresponding European royalty, giving, of course, the preference to the home-manufactured article: it was good to read their raptures over the gallant bearing of Master Lincoln, as if 'the young Iulus' (as they *would* call him) had shown himself worthy of high hereditary honours. One writer, I think, did allow, that the balance of grace might incline rather to Eugénie the Empress, than to the President's stout, good-tempered spouse; but he was much more cynical or conscientious than most of his fellows.

Thenceforward one became aweary of the sight, sound, and name of 'Hooker.' The right man was in the right place at last: had his counsels been followed in the Peninsula, when the caution or incapacity of M'Clellan threw the grand opportunity away, the Federal flag would have floated over Richmond last summer. Was there not the hero's own testimony to that effect, rendered before the War Committee, months ago, wherein, with a chivalrous generosity, he ceased not to exalt himself on the ruined reputation of his late commander? Even as Ajax prayed for light, the people cried aloud for one week of fair weather:

no more was wanted to crush and utterly confound the hopes of Rebels, Copperheads, and perfidious Albion. Every illustrated journal was crowded with portraits, of Fighting Joe and his famous white charger ; it was said, that horse and rider could never show themselves without eliciting a burst of cheering, such as rang out near the Lake Regillus, when Herminius and Black Auster broke into the wavering battle. No wonder. Had he not thoroughly reorganised the army demoralised by Burnside's defeat, till there was but one word in every soldier's mouth, and that word—'Forward'?

There was joy, as for a victory, when it was known that the Falmouth camp was broken up, and that the eager battalions had left the Rappahannock fairly behind them: as to success, only fools or traitors could question it. Even the Democratic journals were carried away by the tide, and hardly ventured to hesitate their doubts. The hero's own proclamation, issued on the south bank of the river, was surely enough to reassure the most timid unbeliever.

How vaunt and prophecy were fulfilled, all the world knows now. A more miserable waste of apparently ample means and material has seldom been recorded in the annals of modern war. General Hooker stands forth the worthy rival of that mighty monarch, who,

> 'With fifty thousand men,
> Marched up the hill and then—marched down again.'

Q

But of the two the exploit of the American strategist is much the most brilliant and memorable; his preparations and blunders were conducted on a vaster scale, and, Varus-like, scorning the triviality of a bloodless disgrace, he left 16,000 dead, wounded, and missing behind in his retreat.

The defeated general may well pray to be saved from his friends: the strongest grounds of condemnation might be drawn from the excuses of some of these injudicious partisans. Not more than a third of the Federal forces was, they say, at any one time engaged: yet Hooker's last words to his troops, before going into action, boasted that the enemy must, perforce, fight him on his own ground. The Federal commander recognised, perhaps not less than his opponent, the importance of the simple old tactic —bringing a superior force to bear on detached or weak points of the adverse line—which has entered, under one form or another, into most great military combinations since war became a science; but he appears to have been utterly incapable of reducing theory to practice. For the twentieth time in this war, a Northern general was out-manœuvred and beaten, simply because his adversary—understanding how to husband an inferior strength—seized the right moment for bringing it into play.

I do not mean to assert that the Confederates invariably advance in column, or to advocate this especial mode of attack: a successful outflanking of

the enemy may turn out an advantage not less
decided than the breaking of his centre; but, when
half-disciplined troops are to be handled, concentrative movements must surely be safer than extensive
ones. It would be well to remember that, among
all the trained battalions of Europe, our own crack
regiments are supposed to be the only ones that can
be thoroughly relied on for attacking in line.

If Hooker thought himself strong enough to cross
the rear of Lee's army, and cut him off from Richmond, while a combined movement against the city
was being executed by Dix and Keyes from the
south-east, the delay of forty hours, during which
he advanced about six miles, can scarcely be excused, or even accounted for. That the wary foe
should be taken entirely by surprise, was a con-
tingency too improbable to be calculated on by
any sane tactician, however sanguine. To dispense
almost entirely with the aid of the cavalry arm,
on the eve of a general engagement, was certainly
a bold stroke of strategy—too bold to be justified
by any independent successes likely to be achieved
by the detachment. Stoneman's exploits appear
to have been greatly exaggerated; but, whatever
were the results, they might clearly have been attained if he had crossed the Rappahannock alone
with his horsemen, leaving the main-guard to attend
more dress-parades in the Falmouth camp. To pretend that weather in anywise influenced Hooker's

retreat, is utterly absurd. No change for the worse took place till the Tuesday evening, when the army had fallen back on the river-bank; the troops were actually re-crossing when the rain began : then it did come down in earnest.

Nocte pluit totâ, redeunt spectacula manè :

—a spectacle, frequently repeated in this war—that of a Federal general 'changing his base' in hot haste, without flourish of trumpet.

At the most critical moment, Fighting Joe seems to have been afflicted with the fatal indecision, by no means incompatible with perfect physical fearlessness, which has ruined wiser plans than ever were moulded in his brain. Rumour hints broadly at a sudden fit of depression, not unnatural in one notoriously addicted to the use of stimulants; but this is, probably, the ill-natured invention of an enemy.

At all such seasons, some subordinate must needs lift some of the dishonour from the shoulders of the chief. The non-arrival of reinforcements, is much the easiest way of accounting for a foiled combination. The rout of Howard's corps was not to be considered, as it happened under the general's own eye : so Sedgwick was, by some, made the Grouchy of the day : but he seems to have fought his division as well as any of his fellows, and it was probably a superior force that checked his advance towards the main army, and eventually hurled him back upon the Rappahannock.

Perhaps the Confederate organs do not greatly exaggerate, when they claim Chancellorville as *the* victory of this war ; though there is a fearful counterpoise in the loss of the South's favourite leader. But the great Army of the Potomac, in its shameful retreat, could not console itself by the boast of having done to death the terrible enemy, at whose name they had learnt to tremble. A miserable mistake (so the Richmond papers say) slew Stonewall Jackson, in the crisis of victory, with a Confederate bullet, as he was reconnoitring with his staff in front of his line.

Surely it is glory, sufficient for any one of woman born, that the news of his death should have sent a start and a shiver through thirty millions of hearts. Not only was there grief and wailing throughout the country that the stern, pure soldier served so well; but a strange honour and respect attaches to his memory, amongst those whom in life he never ceased to disquiet. Even the rabid Republican journalists rejoiced—not coarsely or ungenerously—speaking with bated tones, as is fit and natural in presence of a good man's corpse.

Let us return to our poor Hooker, who is sitting now, somewhat gloomily, in the shade. Human nature can spare so little sympathy for braggarts in disaster, that we may possibly have been too hard

on his demerits.   In this respect the Grim old Fighting Cox (as the historian of the Mackerel Brigade
calls him) is absolutely incorrigible.   Conceive a
general—on the very morning after the reverse was
consummated—proclaiming to his soldiers ' that they
had added to the laurels already won by the Army of
the Potomac!'   If a succession of defeats are equal
to one victory—on the principle of two negatives
making an affirmative—or if nothing added to a
cipher brings out a substantial product, there may
possibly be something in these words beyond the
desperation of bombast, otherwise——

But, in justice to Joseph, let us ask—Are the
materials at his command, or at that of any Federal
commander, really so powerful or manageable as they
seem ?

Probably no one civilised nation is composed of
elements, so difficult to mould into the form of a
thoroughly organised army, as the Northern States
of the Union.   The men individually, especially those
drawn from the West, are fully endowed with the
courage, activity, and endurance inherent in the Anglo-
Saxon race : they can act promptly and daringly
enough, on their own independent resources ; but,
when required to move as unreasoning units of a
mass directed by a superior will, they utterly fail.
All the antecedents of the Federal recruit interfere
with his progress towards the mechanical perfection
of the trained soldier.   The gait and demeanour of

the country lads are not more shambling and slovenly than those of the ordinary British; but the latter from his youth up, has imbibed certain ideas of subordination to superiors, which make him yield more pliantly and implicitly to after-discipline. Now, the American is taught to contemn all such old-world ideas as respect of persons. Even the All-mighty Dollar cannot command deference, though it may enforce obedience. The volunteer carries with him into the ranks, an ostentatious spirit of self-assertion and independence. He has always mixed on terms of as much equality as his purse would allow of, with the class from which his officers have emerged by election; and knows that, at the expiration of their service, each will resume his place as if no such distinction had existed. So he goes into action fully prepared to criticise the orders of his superiors, and even to ignore them if they clash too strongly with his private judgment; he has no intention of abating one iota of his franchise, or one privilege of an enlightened citizen. In the regular army, ceremonial is rather better observed; but, even here, you will observe the barriers of grade frequently transgressed, both in manner and tone: the volunteers will rarely salute even a field-officer, unless on parade, or by special orders.

This spirit of independent judgment, is by no means confined to the rank-and-file. The evidence before the War-Committee shows how seldom a

General-in-Chief can depend on the hearty co-operation of his division-leaders, and how unreservedly
dissent was often expressed by those whose lips discipline ought to have sealed.

The fact is, that a spirit of party impregnates all
the military organisation of the North: a Federal
army is a vast political machine. State Governors
have followed the example of the Administration in
their selection of the higher officers : these, as a rule,
owe their election entirely to their own influence, or
that of their friends ; all other qualifications are dis-
regarded. It is idle to expect that such men can command the confidence of the soldiers by virtue of their
rank ; they have to win this by individual prowess.*
The Confederates have been more just and wise.
Some of these political appointments were made at
the beginning of the war ; but changes were made
as soon as incapacity was manifest ; almost all posts
of importance are now occupied by officers, educated at West Point, or at one of the many military schools long established in the South.

An army of free-thinkers is very hard to handle,
either in camp or field. They do not grumble,
perhaps, so much as the British ' full private ;' indeed

* It is well to remember, that, before the Committee for en-
quiring into the conduct of the war, Generals Mc Dowell and
Rosecrans, in the most explicit terms, attributed many disasters to
the fact, of the soldiers having no confidence in the officers who led
them.

they have little cause, for the commissariat arrangements, even in remote departments, are admirable,
and the Union grudges no comfort, or even luxury,
to her armies. But they become 'demoralised' (the
word is a cant one now) surprisingly fast, and recover
from such depression very, very slowly. When the
moment for action arrives, such men get fresh heart
in the first excitement, but they lack stability, and if
any sudden check ensues, involving change of ground
to the rear, a few minutes are enough to turn a retreat
into a rout. You may send forth your volunteer,
with all the pomp and circumstance of war, and greet
his return with all enthusiasm of welcome ; you may
make him the hero of paragraph and tale (I believe it
is treasonable to choose any other *jeune premier* for a
love-story just now) ; you may put a flag into his
hand, more riddled and shot-torn than any of our old
Peninsular standards ; you may salute him 'veteran,'
a month after the first baptism of fire ; but the savour
of the conscript and the citizen will cling to him still.

What would you have ? The *esprit de corps*, which
has more or less been kept alive in civilised armies
since the days of the Tenth Legion, is, perforce,
wanting here. All military organisation is posterior
to the War of Independence. It is certainly not their
fault if even the regular battalions can inscribe on
their colours no nobler name than that of some desultory Mexican or Border battle. If Australia should
become an empire, she must carry the same blank

ensigns without shame. But, when a regiment has no traditionary honours to guard, it lacks a powerful deterrent from self-disgrace.

It is easy to deride martinets and pipe-clay : all the drill in Christendom will not make a good soldier out of a weakling or a coward ; but, unless you can turn men into machines, so far as to make them act independently of individual thought or volition, you can never depend on a body of non-fatalists for advancing steadily, irrespective of what may be in their front, nor for keeping their ranks unbroken under a hail of fire, or on a sinking ship. As skirmishers, the Federal soldiers act admirably; and in several instances have carried fortified positions with much dash and daring ; it is in line of battle, on a stricken field, that they are—to say the least—uncertain. In spite of highly-coloured pictures of charges, I do not believe that, from the very beginning of this war, any one battalion has actually *crossed* bayonets with another, though they may often have come within ten yards of collision. This fact (which I have taken some trouble to verify) is surely sufficiently significant.

The parallels of our own Parliamentary army, and of the French levies after the first Revolution, suggest themselves naturally here ; but they will not quite hold good. The stern fanatics who followed Cromwell went to their work—whether of fighting or prayer—with all their heart and soul and strength ; conning the manual not less studiously than the psalter, while their general would devote himself for days together to the minutest duties of a drill-sergeant. With all this, and with all his 'trust in Providence,' it was long before the wary Oliver would bring his Ironsides fairly face to face,

With the bravos of Alsatia and the pages of Whitehall.

It is true that the Revolutionary army of '93 was utterly different from those, wherein the Maison du Roi took the right of the line. It was hastily raised, and loosely constructed, out of rude material perilous to handle. But—putting aside that military aptitude inherent in every Frenchman—in all ranks there was a leaven of veterans strong enough to keep the turbulent conscripts in order, though the aristocratic element of authority was wanting. Traditions of sub-ordination and discipline survived in an army, not the less thoroughly French, because it was rabidly Repub-lican. The recruits liked to feel themselves soldiers; they were willing to give up for awhile the pageantry of war, but not its decorum; and, in that implicit obedience to their officers, there mingled a sturdy plebeian pride; they would not allow, that it was harder to follow the wave of Colonel Bonhomme's sabre, than that of Marshal de Montmorenci's bâton; or that the word of command rang out more effi-ciently from the patrician's dainty lips, than from under the rough moustaches of the proletarian.

The regular army here does little to help the

volunteer service, beyond giving subalterns as field-officers; (a lieutenant would rarely be satisfied with a troop or a company); the rank is, of course, temporary, though sometimes substantiated by brevet. It is possible, that a few non-commissioned officers may be found, who have served in a similar or subordinate capacity in the regular army during the Mexican war; but such exceptions are too rare to affect the civism of the entire force.

True it is, that the Federal levies have to face enemies not a whit superior in discipline. Indeed, Harry Wynd's motto, 'I fight for mine own hand,' is especially favoured in the South. But, when one side is battling for independence, the other for subjugation, there must ever be an essential difference in the spirit animating their armies. The impetuosity of the Confederate onset is acknowledged even here: on several occasions it has been marked by a wild energy and recklessness of life, worthy to be compared with the Highland charge, which swept away dragoon and musketeer at Killiecrankie and Prestonpans.

I am not disposed to question the hardihood or endurance of the Yankee militant; nor even to deny that a sense of patriotism may have much to do with his dogged determination to persevere, now, even to the end: but as for enthusiasm—you must look for it in the romances of war that crowd the magazines, or in the letters of vividly imaginative correspondents, or—anywhere but among the Federal rank-and-file.

Such a feeling is utterly foreign to the national character; nor have I seen a trace of it in any one of the many soldiers with whom I have spoken of the war. All the high-flown sentiment of the *Times* or *Tribune*, will not prevent the Yankee private from looking at his duty in a hard, practical, business-like way; he is disposed to give his country its money's worth, and does so, as a rule, very fairly; but military ardour in the States is not exactly a consuming fire at this moment. The hundred-dollar bounty has failed for some time to fill up the gaps made by death or desertion: and the strong remedy of the Conscription Act will not be employed a day too soon. Perhaps those who augur favourably for Northern success expect, that coerced levies will fight more fiercely and endure more cheerfully than the mustered-out volunteers. *Qui vivra verra.*

It is simple justice, to allow that the native soldiers have borne themselves, as a rule, better than the aliens. The Irish Brigade—reduced to a skeleton, now, by the casualties of two years—has performed good service under Meagher, who himself has done much to redeem the ridicule incurred in early days; but the Germans have not been distinguished either for discipline, or daring. The Eleventh Division whose shameful rout at Chancellorville is still in every one's mouth, was almost exclusively a 'Dutch' corps.

But other difficulties beset a Federal general,

besides the intractability of his armed material, and
the jealousies of immediate subordinates.   The uncertainty of his position is in itself a snare.   When the
chief is first appointed, no panegyric seems adequate
to his past merit, and the glories are limitless that
he is certain to win.   If he should inaugurate his
command with the shadow of a success, the Government organs chant themselves hoarse in praise and
prophecy.   But the popular hero knows right well,
that the ground is already mined under his feet ;
the first reverse will drag him down into a pit
of obscurity—if not of odium—deep and dark as
Abiram's grave.   Of all taskmasters, a Democracy is
the most pitilessly irrational ; it were better for an
unfaithful or unlucky servant to fall into Pharaoh's
hands, than to lie at the mercy of a free and enlightened people.   Demagogues, and the crowds they
sway, are just as impatient and impulsive now, as
when the mob of the Agora cheered the bellowing
of Cleon ; neither is their wrath less clamorous
because it has ceased to lap blood.   A Federal chief
must be very sanguine or very short-sighted, who,
beyond the glare and glitter of his new head-quarters,
does not mark the loom of Cynoscephalæ.   Conceive
the worry, of feeling yourself perpetually on your
promotion—of knowing, that by delay you risk the
imputation of cowardice or incapacity, while on the
first decisive action must be perilled the supremacy,
that all men are so loath to surrender.   The unhappy

commander, if a literate, might often think of Por-
sena's front-rank at the Bridge, when

> Those in the rear cried, Forward,
> Those in the van cried, Back.

To few minds is allotted such a temperate and steady
strength, as would enable a man, thus tried and
tempted, to weigh all chances calmly; determined
to strike, only when the time should come; disregarding the extravagant expectations alike of friend
or foe; shrinking no more from the responsibi-
lities of unavoidable failure, than from any other
personal dangers. If such a chief could once fairly
grasp the staff of command, a virtual dictatorship
might work great things for the North. But whence
is he likely to emerge? Hardly from the midst of
this vast political and military turmoil, where every
man is struggling and straining to clutch at the
veriest shred of power.

Hooker has fared better than his fellows in misfortune. The Washington Cabinet, usually ready
enough to make sacrifices to popular indignation,
still stand by their discomfited favourite with creditable firmness. Even before the army crossed the
river, there appeared significant articles in the
Government organs, begging the public to be patient
and moderate in anticipation. The press-prophets,
who indulged in the most magnificent sketches of
what *ought* to be done, were those, with whose

patriotic regrets over defeat, would mingle some exultation over a disgraced political opponent. So, people in general seem content to give the Fighting One another chance.

This unusual clemency may be easily accounted for. It would be almost impossible to pitch on any one with the slightest pretensions to fill the vacated post. If you except Rosecrans, and perhaps Franklin, there is hardly a division-leader who has not, at one time or another, betrayed incapacity enough to dis-qualify him from holding any important command.* West Point may send forth as good theoretical soldiers as Sandhurst, or St. Cyr, while the practical experience of American generals might equal that of our own officers before the Crimean war: but the best from West Point have gone southward long ago, and by the retirement of M'Clellan the North lost, probably, her one promising strategist. Cool and provident in the formation of his plans, though somewhat unready in their execution, and scarcely equal to sudden emergencies,—if he achieved no brilliant success, he was likely to steer clear of grave disaster. The dearth of tacticians is made very

---

* It is somewhat remarkable, that General Grant, who lately achieved a really important success at Vicksburg, was, throughout the winter and spring, the object of the strongest animadversions of the majority of the war-critics; it is true that he had once narrowly escaped a court-martial: nothing but the strong bias of the President in his favour prevented his dismissal from the com-mand of the army of the Mississippi.

manifest, by the list of candidates suggested in the event of Hooker's removal from command.

There are horses, invariably beaten in public, which never appear without being heavily backed; and there are men, who contrive to retain a certain number of partisans, zealous enough to ignore all patent demerits, and to give their favourite credit for any amount of possible unproved capacity. Yet one would have thought the Republicans might have hesitated in bringing forward Fremont, who has already been removed for blunders hardly to be excused by ignorance; and though the name of Sickles is, unhappily, well known in Europe, it is somewhat startling, to find him, so early in the day, an aspirant to the highest military honours. His advocate admits that the latter hero's professional opportunities have been scanty, but, says he, placidly, " Neither was Cæsar bred a soldier." If the sentence was written in sobriety, no praise can be too high for the audacity of that superb comparison. Another patriot was exceedingly anxious that General Halleck should be incontinently removed from the War Office, to make room for—Butler. We accept these things calmly now; for repeated proof has taught us, that world-wide infamy bars no man's road to profit and honour, when Black Republicans weigh the merits of the claimant. The Abolitionist organs of that same week contained glowing accounts of McNeil's exploits in Missouri, and announced with

R

much satisfaction an accession to Negley's brigade in the shape of Colonel Turchin. I quote the words : " He was received with great delight, and will, no doubt, do good service, if allowed. It will be remembered, that he was court-martialled some time since, for punishing guerillas."

Atrocities have been so rife here of late, that even wholesale murder and ravishment have a chance of being lost in the crowd : in any other civilised land than this, that reminder might well have been spared.

Surely the Confederates in the South-west have two prizes now before them, well worth the winning : but in the front of battle Tarquin is seldom found; and, in the rout, they must ride far and fast who would reach his shoulders with the steel. The real perils of these men will begin when the war is done ; the hot Southern *vendetta* will cool strangely, if all the Three shall die in their beds.

[It is almost needless to say that this chapter was written in the Old Capitol. Nothing has occurred since to induce me to alter any of its contents; except that, since Hooker's resignation, I have regretted one or two remarks applied to him, on the old English principle of ' Never hit a man when he's down.']

CHAPTER XIII.

THE DEBATABLE GROUND.

THERE is one very vexed question, the importance of which, both in the present and for the future, can hardly be over-estimated. It does not depend on the vicissitudes, the duration, or even the termination of the war; rather it will become more gravely complicated as prospects of peace dawn clearer.

In which direction do the sympathies and interests of the Border States actually trend?

Let it be understood that the point to be decided is —not whether the Democrats in those parts are politically stronger than their Republican opponents; but whether the popular feeling identifies itself with North or South; whether an uncoerced vote of the majority would be in favour of or hostile to the Union; finally, on which side of the frontier-line, in case of separation, the State would fain abide.

It seems to me, that only personal knowledge and experience can enable an alien to form any accurate opinion on these points; even where the Press is not forced to grumble out discontent with bated breath under terror of martial law, party spirit runs so high

as to render statements, written or spoken, barely
reliable : sound, deeply as you will, into these turbid
wells, it is a rare chance if you touch Truth, after all.
So, of Tennessee, Missouri, or Kentucky, I will not
say a word ; but, for the same reasons, I *may* venture
to hazard more than a guess at the sympathies of
Maryland.

Notwithstanding her superficial extent is comparatively small, there can be no question which of
the Border States enters most importantly into the
calculations of both the belligerent powers ; the
weight of interests and wealth of resources that
Maryland carries with her—to say nothing of her
local advantages—are such that she cannot eventually
be allowed to adhere to either side with a lukewarm
or divided fidelity.

The position I am about to advance will meet with
a certain amount of dissent, if not of incredulity, and
some one will probably point at recent events as furnishing an unanswerable contradiction to much that I
affirm.   I will only pray my readers to believe, that
I have tried hard to cast prejudice aside in listening,
in marking, and in recording ; my opportunities of
forming a deliberate judgment on the sympathies of
all classes in this especial State were such as have
fallen to the lot of very few strangers ; and my obser-
vations *ought*, certainly, to have been the more accurate
from their field having been necessarily narrowed.
Perhaps I can hardly do better than reprint here the

larger portion of a letter, written in the middle of last March, to the " Morning Post ; " nothing that has occurred since induces me materially to modify any one of the opinions expressed therein. Though, in common with many others, I may have regretted the disappointment of our anticipations with regard to a general rising, in co-operation with the Southern invaders, I think it is easy to show that there were reasons sufficient to account for, if not excuse, this second apparent supineness.

" I believe that at home people have a very faint— perhaps a very false—idea of how men think, and act, and suffer in this same Border State. Your impression may be that a lethargy prevails, where, in reality, dangerous fever is the disease—a fever that must one day break out violently, in spite of the quack medicines administered by an incapable Government—in spite of the restrictions unsparingly employed by that grim sick-nurse, martial law.

" I fancy the world is hardly aware of the hearty sympathy with the South—the intense antipathy to the North—which animates at this moment the vast majority of Marylanders. I have heard more than one assert that of the two alternatives, he would infinitely prefer becoming again a colonial subject of England to remaining a member of the Federal Union. This sounds like an exaggeration; I believe it to have been simply the truth, strongly stated. I believe that the partisan spirit is as rife and as bitter in

many parts of this State, as it can be in South
Carolina or Georgia.

" A remarkable instance of this popular feeling
occurred last week, at a large sale in Howard
County. The late proprietor, an Irishman by
descent, belonging to one of the old Roman Catholic
families that have been territorial magnates here for
generations, had a great fancy for dividing his land
into small holdings, rented by men of proportionately
small means, so as to establish a sort of English
tenant-system, involving, of course, much free labour.
It would have been hard to select a spot in that
country where the Abolition feeling would be more
likely to prevail. On the present occasion about
600 farmers and others were assembled. They were
Secessionists to a man ; at least, no one hinted at
dissent when Jeff. Davis's health and more violent
Southern toasts were drunk amidst a storm of cheers.

"Twice has Maryland been taunted with supineness,
if not charged with deliberate treachery ; first when,
at the outbreak of the war, she did not openly secede ;
again, when she did not second by a general rising
Lee's invasion of her boundary. It would be well to
remember, that for Maryland to declare herself, before
Virginia had actually done so, would have been the
insanity of rashness. She could hardly be expected to
defy the vengeance of the North, while cut off by a
neutral State from Southern aid ; especially since
Governor Hicks's measures of disarmament, by which

not only the militia but private individuals were deprived of their firelocks. Virginia has fought so gallantly since then, that it is easy to forget her tardiness in drawing the sword ; but it would be vain to deny that on the Southern bank of the Potomac there does exist a certain jealousy, arising probably from conflicting commercial interests, which has led to suspicion and misconception already, and may lead to more harm yet. General Lee issued his proclamation inviting Maryland to rise only one day before he commenced his retreat—short notice, surely, for a revolution involving not only the temporary ruin of many interests, but the certainty of collision with a Federal army of 120,000 men then within the border of the State. Had Maryland joined the Confederacy a year ago, I believe her entire territory would be desolate now, as are most great battle-fields. With the immense means of naval transport at the Federals' command, it would be easy for them to land any number of troops in almost any part of the western division, for the whole country is intersected by the creeks of the Chesapeake Bay and its tributary rivers. One glance at the map will show this more plainly than verbal description, and make it needless to remark on the still more exposed and isolated position of the eastern shore.

"In spite of all this, men say that if the opportunity were once more given, the blade would be drawn in earnest, and the scabbard thrown away.

It may well be so; there has been oppression and provocation enough of late to make the scale turn once and for ever.

"Meantime, Maryland has not confined herself to a suppressed sympathy with the South. We may guess, perhaps, but no one will ever know, the extent of the covert assistance already rendered by this State to the Confederacy. I am not referring to the constant reinforcements of her best and bravest— over 12,000, it is said—that have never ceased to feed the ranks of the Southern armies. (One significant fact is worth mentioning, drawn from the reports of Federal officers—viz., out of 9,000 Marylanders drafted into the service, there are scarcely 100 now remaining in the ranks; they deserted, literally, by bands.)

"I speak of supplies of all sorts, especially medicines, furnished perpetually; of valuable information forwarded as to the enemy's movements and intentions; of Confederate prisoners tended with every care, and supplied with every comfort that womanly tenderness could devise; of a hundred other marks of substantial friendship that could not only be rendered by a nominal neutral, but a real ally. It would be hard indeed if any miserable jealousies were to prevent all this from being appreciated and rewarded some day.

"The Federal Government, at least, does ample justice to the proclivities of Maryland. The system

of coercion, hourly more and more stringent, speaks
for itself. The State is at this moment subjected to
a military despotism more irritating and oppressive
than was ever exercised by Austria in her Italian
dependencies; more irritating, because domestic interference and all sorts of petty annoyances are more
frequent here; more oppressive, because it is considered unnecessary to indulge a political prisoner
with even the mockery of a trial.

Nothing is too small for the gripe of the Provost-
Marshal's myrmidons. There was a general order last
week for the seizure of all Southern songs and photo-
graphs of Confederate celebrities. One convivial cheer
for Jefferson Davis brought the 'strayed reveller' the
following morning into the awful presence of Colonel
Fish, there to be favoured with one of his characteristic diatribes. The duties of that truculent potentate are doubtless both difficult and disagreeable, yet
one would think it possible for an officer to act
energetically without ignoring the common courtesies
of life, and to maintain rigid discipline without constantly emulating the army that 'swore terribly in
Flanders.' The Oath of allegiance—that is the touch-
stone, whose mark gives everything its marketable
value. The Union flag must wave over every spot—
chapel, mart, institute, or ball-room—where two or
three may meet together; beyond the shadow of
the enforced ensign there is little safety or comfort
for man, woman, or child—for woman least of all.

"During the past week, two ladies of this city have been arraigned on the charge, of aiding and abetting deserters from the Federal army. In the first case, the offence was having given a very trifling alms, after much solicitation and many refusals, to a man who represented himself and his family as literally starving. The fugitive made his way to Canada, and thence wrote two begging‑letters, threatening, if money were not sent, to denounce his benefactress. Eventually he did so. This lady is to be separated from her husband and family, with whom she is now residing, and sent across the lines in a few days. In the second case I am justified in mentioning names, as from the peculiar circumstances it will probably become more public. Mrs. Grace is the widow of an Havana merchant, and a naturalised subject of Spain, to whose Minister she has since appealed. She was summoned before the Provost-Marshal on the same charge, but was too ill to attend in person. Her daughter went to the office, and found that the evidence against her mother was an intercepted letter from some person (whose name was equally unknown to Mrs. Grace as to the officials), telling his wife 'to go to that lady, who would take care of her.' Miss Grace represented the extreme hardship of the case; they had no friends or connections in the South, and her mother's health was far from strong. Finally, she gave her own positive assurance that there was not the faintest foundation for the charge. Colonel

Fish did not scruple to reply, that he considered an anonymous document evidence strong enough to bear down a lady's proffered word of honour. If, after this provocation, the spirit of the fair pleader was roused, and she spoke somewhat unadvisedly with her lips, few will be disposed to impute to her anything more than imprudence. The Provost-Marshal closed the discussion very promptly and decidedly—'Your mother will go South within the fortnight; and you, for your insolence, will accompany her.' When women and weaklings are before them, the *argumentum baculinum* seems favoured by the Republican chivalry.

"The country is not much better off than the city. The same system of espionage and coercion prevails there; especially since that fatal Proclamation has sown distrust between master and slave, it is hard to say how many spies there may be in any man's household. Large landed proprietors, who have shown no sign of Southern proclivity, beyond abstaining from taking the Oath, cannot obtain the commonest necessaries, such as groceries, &c., without resorting to shifts and stratagems that would be absurd, if they were not so painful. Such trammels are far more galling to the purely agricultural class than they are to the inhabitants of a city like this, where commerce has introduced a large mixed element, embracing not only Northerners, but almost every European race.

"But, in spite of all privations and annoyances, there

is in the Marylander, just now, an honest earnestness
of purpose, a readiness for self-sacrifice, a patient
hardihood, a brave, hopeful spirit, quick to chafe but
slow to complain, that might make Anglo-Saxons feel
proud of their common blood.   There is plenty of
the stuff left out of which Buchanan, Semmes, Maffit
(of the Florida), Hollins, and Kelso are made—
Marylanders all—who are doing their *devoir* gallantly
on the decks of Southern war-ships.   I cannot believe
that the day is far distant, when both moral and
physical energy will have free and fair play.

" The ties of mutual interest that bind this State to
the Confederacy are too obvious to need much explanation, but it may be well to touch upon them briefly.
Her extensive water-power marks out Maryland as
eminently adapted for the produce of all kinds of
manufactures.   That very accessibility from seaward
which is her weak point in war time, is her strength
in time of peace.   The Chesapeake and its tributaries
are natural high roads for the transport of freight
to the ports of Virginia, and thence into the interior.
Before these troubles, the trade of Maryland was
almost exclusively with the South; and, unless
violently diverted, it must always remain so.   The
South is now straining every nerve to establish a
formidable steam-navy.   It is not too much to say
that the adhesion of Maryland is absolutely indispen-
sable if this object is to be attained.   She can not
only offer superb harbours, in which the South is

palpably deficient, but her natural productions—ship timber, iron ore (the largest and toughest plates in the United States are hammered here), and bituminous coal, the best for steam purposes south of Nova Scotia—would be invaluable.

With this State the South would retain all the material advantages that the restoration of the Union could offer ; without her, neither would the territorial line be complete, nor the internal resources adequate to the requirements of a powerful nation. President Davis has repeatedly promised that the free vote of Maryland as to her future shall be one of the prime conditions of any treaty whatsoever, and the Southern Congress have confirmed this by a nearly unanimous vote. On this point there surely ought to be no doubt or wavering. A single concession to the arbitrary tendencies of Lincoln's Cabinet, so as to allow interference with the free expression of Maryland's will when the crisis shall arrive, would not only, I believe, crush the hopes of the vast majority of this State's inhabitants, but also betray the vital interest of the Southern Confederacy in days to come."

If further proof were needed of the Southern sympathy prevalent in Baltimore, such would be found in the measures of coercion and prevention, employed by General Schenck, when Lee's army was thought dangerously near. A private letter, despatched to me in the height of the panic, more than confirmed the accounts in public prints of the stringency of the martial law. The Federal officers were, perhaps, not sorry to have such a chance of repaying, with aggravated oppression, the tacit contumely which must have galled them for a year and more. The Maryland Club, whose members are Southerners to a man (for the Unionist element was eliminated long ago), is now the head-quarters of a New England regiment, and even Colonel Fish may now wander at will through the cool, pleasant chambers that, before comparative liberty was stifled, he would have found not more accessible than the lost paradise of Sultan Zim. I greatly fear that some of those daring dames and damsels, so careless in dissembling their antipathies, may, ere this, have been made to pay a heavy price for the indulgence of past disdain. The position of a Federal officer, in Baltimore, was certainly far from enviable; many men would have preferred the lash of a cutting-whip, or even a slight flesh-wound, to the sidelong glances that, when a dark-blue uniform passed by, interpreted so eloquently the fair Secessionists' repugnance and scorn. Neither were words always wanting to convey a covert insult. I heard rather an amusing instance of this while I was in prison.

It was at the time when Brigadier-generals were being created by scores (I myself counted over sixty names sent down by the President to Congress in one batch); when, according to some Washington Pasquin, a stone, thrown at a night-prowling dog in Penn-

sylvania Avenue, struck three of these fresh-fledged
Eagles. A Baltimorian *lionne* had entered one of the
street railway cars, in which two or three Federal officers were already seated: an infantry soldier got in
immediately afterwards, and, in taking his place, set
his boot accidentally on the silken verge of a far-
flowing robe. The lady gazed on the unconscious
offender for a minute or so, and spake no word; then—
looking beyond him as though he had never been—
she addressed the conductor with the pretty plaintive-
ness affected by those languid Southern beauties:

" Sir, won't you ask that Brigadier-general to take
his foot off the skirt of my dress ? "

Which position was the most enviable at that
moment—the 'full private's' or that of his silent
superiors ?

It was curious to remark how thoroughly the majority of clergymen, of all denominations, but especially
Roman Catholic priests, identified themselves with the
Southern sympathies of their flock. Arrests of these
reverend men were very common; but they held on
their way undauntedly, and 'kept silence even from
good words' only under the pressure of actual coercion.
Another anecdote is worth relating.

One day there came forth an edict, peremptory as
that which bade all nations and languages bow down
to a Golden Image, enjoining that, on a certain
Sabbath, prayers for the President should be offered
up in every church, chapel, and meeting-house in

Baltimore. There was an ancient Episcopalian divine, who, during nearly half a century, had won for himself much affection and respect by a zealous and kindly discharge of his duties. A notorious Secessionist, he was wise and prudent withal; so that many were curious to hear, how he would execute or evade the obnoxious order. He complied with it—in this wise:

"My brethren," said he, "we are commanded, this day, to intercede with the Almighty for the President. Let us pray. May the Lord have mercy on Abraham Lincoln's soul."

Did ever priest pronounce a blessing more grimly like a ban?

Perhaps it was well, that Lee did not advance near enough to Baltimore to bring things to a climax, unless he could have succeeded in capturing the place by a *coup de main*, and have held it permanently. Independently of Schenck's avowed intention of shelling the town, on the first symptoms of disaffection, from the forts of Constitution and McHenry, there might have been wild work there in more ways than one. If the Secessionists had once fairly risen against their oppressors and—not prevailed, it is difficult to say, where the measures of savage retaliation would have ended. I do not like to think of the brutality that might have lighted on many hospitable households, in blood-shedding or rapine.

So much for the city. I have mentioned above

some of the reasons, that make an up-rising throughout the State so exceedingly difficult and dangerous
to organise. That no active aid was rendered to Lee's
army upon the last occasion of its crossing the frontier, is, I think, easily explained, when, the peculiar
circumstances of time and place are considered.

Southern proclivity is by no means so general in the
North-western counties of Maryland as in the Eastern
region, or on the sea-board. The farmers in the
former parts suffer greatly from the ceaseless incursions
over the border. When cattle are to be driven away,
it is feared that even regular 'raiders' and guerillas
are not over-careful to ascertain the sympathies of
the owner. The horse-thieves, of course, are absolutely indifferent whether they plunder friend or foe.
Now, though the Marylander is far from being im-
bued with the exclusively commercial spirit of the
Yankee, it is not unnatural that he should chafe
under these repeated assaults on his purse, if not on
his person. All such considerations vanish in the fierce
energy of the thorough partisan, who, without grudg-
ing or remorse, casts the axe-head after the helve;
but I speak, now, of men whose sympathies at the
commencement of the war were almost neutral, and
who began to suffer in the way above described,
before the bias of feeling had time to determine
itself. It was surely natural, that the first angry im-
pulses should turn the wavering scale; more especially
when the irritation was constantly being renewed.

S

Beyond these north-western counties, in neithe
inroad, did the Confederate army advance. I was no
much surprised at reading in the able letter of th
Times correspondent, how the Southerners were dis
appointed by meeting all along their brief line o
march gloomy faces and sullen dislike, instead of ;
hearty welcome; for I knew that in the neighbour
hood of Hagerstown, Boonesborough, and all round
South Mountain, the majority of the inhabitant:
were—to use my Irishman's expression—as ' black a:
thunder.'

One glance at the field of the recent operations wil
show, that the isolated Secessionists in the south-
eastern counties could do little more, than pray for the
success of the Confederate arms; even detached
bodies of such sympathisers could not have joined
Lee, without running the gauntlet of the Federal
forces lying right across the path.

It should not be forgotten, that the stakes of the
invader, and of the insurgent differ widely. The
former, if worsted, can fall back on his own ground
with no other damage than the actual loss sustained
The latter, if foiled, must calculate on absolute ruir
—if not on worse miseries. Even if he should himself escape scathless beyond the frontier, he must
leave homestead and family behind—to be dealt with
as chattels and kindred of traitors.

Thus, though I am disposed to think more despond-
ingly than before of Maryland's chances of aiding

herself, for the present, with the armed hand, my conviction remains unchanged as to the proclivities of the majority of her population, both civic and agricultural. I do honestly believe that, in despite of the tempting geographical water-line, the natural place of the State is in the Southern Confederacy. And I do also believe, that the denial of a free vote as to her future, and a coerced adhesion to the Northern Union, would involve, not only the ruin of many important interests, political and commercial, but an Exodus of more influential residents, than has occurred in any civilised land, since the Revolutionary storm drove thousands of patrician emigrants over every frontier of France.

CHAPTER XIV.

EVERYONE in anywise interested, practically or theoretically, in the Great War, is just now prophesying of the future, simply because it looks vaguer and dimmer than ever. So I will hazard my guess at truth before all is done.

I am no more capable of giving a valid opinion as to the chances or resources of the South than if I had never left these English shores. Proximity that is not positive presence, rather embarrasses one's judgment, for the nearer you approach the frontier-line, the more you become bewildered in the maze of exaggerated reports, direct contradictions, and conflicting statistics. Judging from individual cases and from the spirit animating the 'sympathisers' on the hither side of the border, I feel sure that the bitter determination of the South to hold out to the last man and the last ounce of corn-bread, has not been in the least over-stated; but as to the aspect of chances, or as to the actual loss or gain achieved by either side up to this moment, I am no more qualified to speak than any careful student of the war-chronicles. It is from consideration of the present and probable strength or weakness of Federaldom, that I should draw the grounds of any opinion that I might hazard.

I think *both* are generally under-estimated. In spite of the resistance offered in many places to the Conscription Act, it is likely that for some time to come the North will always be able to bring into the field armies numerically far superior to those of her adversary; nor do I believe that she will have exclusively to depend on raw or enforced levies. Many of the three-year men and others, whose term of volunteer service has just expired, after a brief rest and experience of home monotony, will begin to long for excitement again, though accompanied by peril and hardship. To such, the extravagant bounty will be a great temptation, and the Government may not be far wrong in calculating on the re-enlistment of a large per-centage of the 'veterans.' Besides, it should always be remembered that if it comes to wearing one another out in the drain of life, the preponderance of twenty millions against four must tell fearfully, even though the willingness to serve on the one side, should equal the reluctance on the other. Neither do I think that national bankruptcy is so imminent over the Northern States, as some would have it. Mr. Chase is, of course, a perilously reckless financier; but, on more than one occasion, audacity has served him well, when prudent sagacity could have been of little aid: the 'Five-and-Twenty' Loan was certainly eminently successful, and the tough, broad back of Yankee-land will bear more burdens yet before it breaks or bends. I am speaking now solely of the resources which can be made available for *carrying on* the war: these, I think, will be found sufficient for its probable duration. With the commercial future or national credit of the Northern States this question has nothing to do; it is not difficult to foresee how both must inevitably be compromised by the load of debt which swells portentously with every hour of warfaring. But if we have been wont to undervalue the strength of Federaldom, latent and displayed, we have perhaps scarcely realised how very unsubstantial and slippery are its presumed points of vantage.

First take the North great battle or, rather, stalking-horse—Abolition.

Let no reader be here unnecessarily alarmed. On that terrible slave question, over which wiser brains have puzzled, till they became lost in a labyrinth of self-contradiction, I purpose to speak only a few cursory words. It is beyond dispute that a vast extent of the richest land in the South can only be kept in cultivation by the Africans, who can thrive and fatten where the white man withers helplessly. No one that has realised the present state of our own West Indian colonies, will believe that the enfranchised negro can be depended upon as a daily labourer for hire. The listless indolence inherent in all tropical races *will* assert itself, as soon as free agency begins or is restored. With a bright sun overhead, and a sufficiency of sustenance for the day, before him, money will not tempt Sambo to toil among cotton or canes, should the spirit move him to lie under his own vine or fig-tree ; and he is unfortunately peculiarly liable to these lazy fits just when his services are most vitally important to the interests of his employer. From so much ground having been thrown out of cultivation in the West Indies, the supply of free negro labour is perhaps now nearly equal to the ordinary demand ; but we all know how in the early times of emancipation, the fortunes of our planters fared. There has been, in all ages, certain cases of apparent political necessity, hardly to be justified— sometimes hardly to be defended—on purely moral grounds. Whether the existence and maintenance of a slave population in the South be one of these huge dilemmas or paradoxes is a question that any English or Northern abolitionist is about as capable of deter- mining, as he would be of legislating for Mongolian Tartary.

The two blackest points in all the dark system— for dark it is, looking at it how you will—are first, the complication of sin and shame arising from the mixture of the races ; and secondly, the separation of husband and wife from each other, and from their infant families, by sale. I do firmly believe that the recurrence of the former evil becomes rarer every day, for advance of civilisation only seems to strengthen the natural repugnance—with which moral sentiment has nothing to do—existing between the Anglo-Saxon and African blood.

The subject is not a pleasant one to dilate upon, but that such a repugnance does exist, few that have been brought into actual contact with the ' coloured ' element *en masse,* will be inclined to deny.   I think some of those scientific philosophers who write volumes to prove that there is no physical difference between the races would feel their theories strangely modified after such a practical trial.   If this be an immutable fact, it may work in the South for the pre-vention of evil as well as of good; in the North it can only work for bitter harm.   In Delaware, where the free negroes are found in unusually large propor-tion to the whites, they are notoriously more hardly treated than in any other State of the original Union ; and fanaticism must be blind and deaf indeed if recent events in New York have not taught it to doubt whether the tender mercies of the Abolitionists are so gentle, after all.   While things are so (and there is scant hope of their changing within many generations) the position of the black freed-man in the North will never be much higher than that of the Chinese in California, where a scintilla of civil rights is the utmost that the unhappy aliens can claim.   In the South, I do greatly fear, there is no alternative between suppression and subjugation.

There is no reason why the second great evil—the separation of families (under a certain age) should not

be entirely removed by proper legislation ; and I
believe measures to this effect have already been
mooted in more than one of the slave-holding States.
Putting these two points aside, I believe that the
condition of the slave — especially where the
' patriarchial ' system prevails,—is infinitely better
than that of the coolies: the unutterable horrors and
the waste of life in the Chincha Islands have never
been matched in Kentucky or Louisiana. I believe
that the whole roll of authenticated cruelties exercised on the negroes in any one year would be outnumbered and out-done by the brutalities practised
within the same time upon the apprentices in our own
coast-trade, and upon seamen—white and coloured—
in the American merchant-service. With all this it
should be remembered that the ordinary slave-rations
far exceed, both in quantity and quality, the Sunday
meal of an English West-country labourer ; and that
the comforts of all the aged and infirm, whom the
master is, of course, obliged to maintain, are infinitely
superior to those enjoyed by the like inmates of our
most lenient workhouses.

I think it is a mistake to suppose that the negroes,
as a race, *pine* for freedom ; though when it is
suggested to them they may grasp at it with eager-
ness, much as they would at any other novelty. Many,
no doubt, can appreciate liberty, and use it as
wisely and well as any free-born white : gradual
emancipation would be one of the grandest schemes

that could be propounded to human benevolence : it is rife with difficulty, but surely not impracticable. The indiscriminate and abrupt manumission of the negro would, I am convinced, turn a quaint, simple, childish creature—prone to mirth, and not easily discontented, if his indolence be not taxed too hardly, susceptible, too, of strong affection and fidelity to his masters, as many recent events have shown—into a sullen, slothful, insolent savage, never remembering the past, except as a sort of vague excuse for the present indulgence of his brutal instincts, conscious that every man's hand is against him, without the meek patience of a pariah; but only venturing to retaliate by occasional outbursts of ruffianism or rapine. Where a body of these men is subjected at once to military discipline, and over-awed by the presence of white soldiers in overwhelming numbers, the same danger cannot exist; yet I doubt gravely as to the ultimate success, in any point of view, of those negro levies. It seems hard to say, but I do think it is better for us—even for the sake off Christian charity—to leave that Great Anomaly to be dealt with by God in His own time.

Were the cause stronger than it is, it would be damaged with many moderate thinkers, by the absurdities and violence of its most zealous advocates. Ward Beecher, the great Abolition apostle, fairly outdoes the earlier eccentricities of Spurgeon; every trick of stage effect—such as the sudden display of a white slave-child—is freely employed in the pulpit of Plymouth Church, and each successful ' point ' is rewarded by audible murmurs of applause. One fact stamps the man very sufficiently. In the latter part of last May, he was starting for a four-months' absence in Europe: it was purely a pleasure trip, the expenses to be paid by 'his affectionate congregation ; ' and the whole arrangements were thoroughly comfortable, not to say luxurious. The text of his last sermon was taken from Acts, ch. xx. vv. 18—27 —words that even an Apostle never spoke till, standing in the shadow of bonds and death, he said farewell to saints who should never more look upon his face.

Theodore Tillon, another shining light, much distinguished himself by announcing that there was no doubt that ' the negroes were destined to be *The* Church of Christ:' he founded his discovery not so much upon the strong religious feeling prevalent among ' coloured ' persons, as on that verse in the Songs of Solomon, where the Bride professes herself ' black but comely !'

It would be well if such absurdities were all one had to record : some ebullitions of abolitionist zeal will hardly bear writing down. Take one instance. At a large Union meeting at Philadelphia, the *Reverend* A. H. Gilbert, speaking of the Proclamation, and its probable effects in the South, did not deny that it might entail a repetition of the San

Domingo horrors on a vaster scale. 'But,' said he, —'speaking calmly and as a Christian minister—I affirm that it would be better that every woman and child in the South should perish, than that the principles of Confederate statesmen should prevail.'

In all that huge assembly there was not one man found who—for the love of wife, or sister, or daughter, or mother,—would rise to smite the brutal blasphemer on the mouth : nay, the Quaker brood cheered him to the echo.

That same Proclamation has done less harm than was expected after all. Maryland has suffered, perhaps, most : the whole constitution is rendered null and void there now, without her gaining any European credit as a voluntary Free State. The negroes stay or run away according to their fancy, and work as it suits their convenience ; the chances against re-capture being about 1000 to 1, so it says something for the system that so many have chosen to remain : hardly any household or domestic servants are found among the fugitives.

Putting Abolition aside, let us examine the condition of the North's 'second charger'—battle-horse—Restoration of the Union at any cost. The question, of the right of the Southern States to secede, has been discussed till every European ear must be weary of the theme ; so we will let the justice of the case alone, and only look at the wild improbability of any such result being achieved. In the North, of course,

there is a strong peace-party ; in the South I do not
think that any man would venture to suggest to his
nearest friend any compromise short of the acknow-
ledgment of the Confederacy as an independent
nation.   It is an utter mistake to suppose that, if the
Emancipatory Proclamation were revoked, the road
towards Peace would be smoothed materially : it
might have a good effect in displaying a spirit of conciliation on the part of the Federal Government—
nothing more.   The wedges that will keep the South
apart from the North, for ever, were moulded and
sharpened long before they were driven home.   For
years far-seeing men, especially on the Border States,
had provided, in their financial and domestic arrangements, for a certain disunion : not for the first time
in history has an aristocracy grown up in the centre
of a democracy, and, while the world shall last, such
a state of things can never long endure without a
collision, involving temporary subjugation or permanent disruption.

The New-Englander sees this just as plainly as the
Virginian, and both have an equal pride in thinking
that Cavalier and Roundhead are fighting the old
battle once more.   Disputes about tariffs and falsified
compromises have only been specious pretexts for
indulging in a spirit of antagonism, which was then
scarcely dissembled, and can never be glossed over
again.   But the Federal Government are not only
pursuing a *mirage*, in trying to enforce an Union

which could scarcely be maintained if all the South
country lay depopulated and desolate : they are risking, every day, more perilously, the cohesion of the
States that still cleave to the old commonwealth.
The Black Republican tendency to put down all political opposition with the armed hand or with the
lettre du cachet, is perpetually conflicting with the
State rights, which many true-hearted Americans
value no less highly than their allegiance to the Union.
The Democrats are almost strong enough to defy their
opponents, even while the latter are in power; and
resistance to the Conscription may be only the beginning of a struggle that will terminate in a second
solution of political continuity, not less earnest than
the first.   Listen to *The World*, of the 19th May,
speaking of Vallandigham's arrest :

" The blood that already makes green, Virginian
and Kentucky hill-sides, is but a drop to that which
will flow on Northern soil, when the American people
discover that the battle has begun to save the Constitution from tyrants."

Brave words, these ! Yet, making allowance for
editorial blatancy, they may contain a germ of bitter
truth.   When New York—the Empress City—has
been threatened with martial law, it is fair to
conclude that Federaldom may soon have other
enemies to deal with than those who are vexing her
borders.

No Government can hope successfully to carry out

the principle of arbitrary and irresponsible power, unless its standing-ground be as unassailable, and its resolves as unanimous as those of any individual autocrat.

Yet, no administration—civil, political, or military —can be otherwise than unsound to the core where no mutual confidence or reliance subsists among its constituent members. Mr. Lincoln's Cabinet do not even keep up the appearances of a Happy Family; in all the subordinate departments, scarcely a week elapses without the promulgation of some disgraceful scandal. For instance, last Spring, before men had had time to discuss the gigantic Custom-house frauds, there appeared a quiet paragraph to the effect that 140,000 dollars had disappeared mysteriously from the Navy Office on the eve of pay-day; a huge reward was offered for the discovery of the criminal, or recovery of the money; but even Unionists laughed openly at such an advertisement, which probably did not cause the real robber, whoever he was, to turn once uneasily in his gorgeous bed. Even in the Commissariat, which, in all ages and in all armies, has been the presumed head-quarters of the Autolyci, no one has yet emulated the evil renown of the Batters at New Orleans (it was openly stated in Congress, and scarcely contradicted, that the profits and plunder carried off by that noble pair of brothers, exceeded seven millions of dollars); but many of the contractors appear to have used their opportunities, much as if they were scrambling for eagles, or robbing 'against time.' The corruption that has long prevailed in Congress, whenever a 'private bill' is in question, has long been notorious; but this, at least, was shrouded with a thin veil of decorum which the peculators in military and civil high places disdained to encumber themselves with in these latter days.

Instances of all this might be multiplied to weariness, but you have only to look at a week's files of any Northern journal to be convinced of the existing state of things, which even the Black Republicans not unfrequently bewail.

There is another sort of extra-horse that the Government, or its organs, are fond of riding for a short 'spell,' when the others have been hacked rather too hardly. They have christened it—'Perfidious Albion.' To speak the truth, however, the Anglophobia is not confined to the Abolitionists or Republicans, when anything occurs to make any particular journal cross or querulous, you are almost sure to meet, that same week, a sanguinary leader, with the threadbare motto — '*Delenda est Britannia.*' Lately, it has been suggested that the most certain means to secure the adhesion of the South, would be an invitation to join in an internecine war with England and France, with Canada and Mexico for prizes.

Truly Secessia has little cause to love us; for our practical sympathy with her in her dire strait, has been confined to the furnishing of war-munitions at a moderate profit of 300 per cent.; yet, I think, even in such a cause, Georgia, Carolina, and Virginia would stand aloof, rather than dress up in line with the Yankee battalions. The mobocracy are 'all for a muss,' of course, as they always are till they see the glitter of bayonets; but I cannot believe that the bellicose ideas they are so fond of mooting, have ever been seriously entertained by the Government. The Federal navy is too utterly inefficent now, save for attack and defence along its own shores, to give cause for apprehension even to a second-class Power : it cannot even protect Northern commerce. For a year or more, the Florida and Alabama have laughed at the beards of all the cruisers, and carry on depredation still with a high hand. The only grave aggression must be made on the frontier of Canada; and there the invaders would be met by a militia quite as well drilled as themselves, who have held their own, once before, gallantly; to say nothing of the reinforcement of our own regular army; if the crack regiments of New York or Massachusetts should chance, in such a case, to find the Guards or Highlanders in their front, it is just possible that the 'veterans' might have some fresh ideas as to the realities of a 'charge in line.'

Reading these bellicose articles, you are perpetually reminded of the favourite national game of 'Poker.' In this, a player holding a very bad hand against a good

T

one, may possibly 'bluff' his adversary down, and win the stakes, if he only has confidence enough to go on piling up the money, so as to make his own weakness appear strength. That audacity answers often happily enough, especially with the timid and inexperienced, but the professional gamblers tell you mournfully that they sometimes meet an opponent with equal nerve and a longer purse, then comes the fatal moment when the cards must be shown, and then—*le quart d'heure de Rabelais.* I think, if ever Britannia is forced to 'see' Federalia's 'hand,' the world that looks on will find that the latter has been 'bluffing' to hide weakness.

Nevertheless, I am far from undervaluing the actual strength of the Northern land-armies. They are composed of the most uncouth and heterogeneous materials; but they work well enough after their own rough fashion, and certainly recover surprisingly fast from temporary discomfiture: it is difficult to believe that the troops who met Lee so gallantly at Gettysburg were the same who recrossed the Rappahannock in sullen despondency, after Chancellorsville. But the foreign element in the Federal forces must soon grow dangerously strong: it should never be forgotten that the foreigners, attracted by enormous bounty, even if they be of Anglo-Saxon blood, can be but mercenaries, after all: and, in history, the Swiss almost monopolise the glory of mercenary fidelity. Such subsidies can only be relied on when pay is prompt and work plenty : irregularity or inaction will soon breed discontent, followed by some such revolt as menaced the existence of Carthage.

These are some of the causes which, as it seems to me, even now neutralise to a great extent the really vast resources of the North, and will some day imperil her very existence as a nation—united in her present form. Now, as to the event of the struggle.

I believe amalgamation, or any other terms than absolute subjugation of the South—to be maintained hereafter by armies of occupancy—simply impracticable. This — not only on the grounds of political and social antagonism before alluded to ; but because this contest has been waged after a fashion almost unknown in the later days of Civilisation. I do not speak of open warfare on stricken fields, or even of pitiless slaughter wrought by those who, when their blood is hot, ' do not their work negligently '; but of bitter bye-blows, dealt on either side, such as humanity cannot lightly forget or forgive—of passions roused, that will rankle savagely long after this generation shall be dust. There remains the chance of utterly quelling and annihilating the insurrection (I speak as a Federal) with the strong hand.

On the one side is ranged an innumerable multitude—who can hardly be looked upon as a distinct nation, for in it mingles all the blood of Western Europe—doggedly determined, perhaps, to persevere in its purpose, yet strangely apathetic when a crisis

seems really imminent—easily discouraged by reverses, and fatally prone to discontent and distrust of
all ruling powers—divided by political jealousies,
often more bitter than the hatred of the Commonwealth's foe—mingling always with their patriotism
a certain commercial calculation, that if all tales are
true, makes them, from the highest to the lowest,
peculiarly open to the temptations of the Almighty
Dollar; these men are fighting for a positive gain,
for the re-acquisition of a vast territory, that if
they win, they must watch, as Russia has watched
Poland.

On the other side I see a real nation, numerically
small, in whose veins the Anglo-Saxon blood flows
almost untainted; I see rich men casting down their
gold, and strong men casting down their lives, as if
both were dross, in the cause they have sworn to
win; I see Sybarites enduring hardships that *un vieux
de la vieille* would have grumbled at, without a
whispered murmur; I hear gentle and tender women
echo in simple earnestness the words that once were
spoken to me by a fair Southern wife—"I pray that
Philip may die in the front, and that they may burn
me in the plantation, before the Confederacy makes
peace on any terms but our own." I see that
reverses, instead of making this people cashier their
generals, or cavil at their rulers, only intensify their
fierce energy of resistance. Here men are fighting—
not to gain a foot of ground, but simply to hold their

own, with the liberty which they believe to be their birthright.

It may well be that darker days are in store for the South than she has ever yet known; it may be that she will only attain her object at the cost of utter commercial ruin; it may be that the charity of the European Powers is exhausted on Poland, and that neither pity nor shame will induce them to break a thankless neutrality, here; but, in the face of all barely probable contingencies, I doubt no more of the ultimate result, than I doubt of the ultimate performance of the justice of God.

THE END.

BRADBURY AND EVANS, PRINTERS, WHITEFRIARS

For EU product safety concerns, contact us at Calle de José Abascal, 56–1°, 28003 Madrid, Spain or eugpsr@cambridge.org.

www.ingramcontent.com/pod-product-compliance
Ingram Content Group UK Ltd.
Pitfield, Milton Keynes, MK11 3LW, UK
UKHW010347140625
459647UK00010B/885